Nelson
Spelling 5

Edgar Schmidt and Catherine Walker

Series Authors

Donna Duplak
Deb Kekewich
Jim Kekewich
Clare Kosnik
Louis Quildon
Edgar Schmidt
Catherine Walker
Clare Kosnik, Senior Author

I(T)P Nelson

an International Thomson Publishing company

Toronto • Albany • Bonn • Boston • Cincinnati • Detroit • London • Madrid • Melbourne
Mexico City • New York • Pacific Grove • Paris • San Francisco • Singapore • Tokyo • Washington

D1299812

I⊤P™
International Thomson Publishing
The trademark ITP is used under licence

© I⊤P™ Nelson Canada,
A Division of International Thomson Limited, 1997
All rights in this book are reserved

Published by Nelson Canada,
A Division of International Thomson Limited
1120 Birchmount Road
Scarborough, Ontario
M1K 5G4

ISBN 0-17-606558-X

Canadian Cataloguing in Publication Data

Schmidt, Edgar
    Nelson Spelling 5

ISBN 0-17-606558-X

1. Spellers.   I. Walker, Catherine (Catherine M.)
II. Title.

PE1145.2.S35 1996   428.1   C96-931464-7

Project Editor: Jennifer Rowsell
Series Editor: Alan Simpson
Series Designer: Peggy Rhodes
Senior Composition Analyst: Marnie Benedict
Cover Illustrator: Stephen MacEachern
Production Coordinator: Donna Brown
Permissions: Vicki Gould
Film: Imaging Excellence
Photography: Ray Boudreau

Printed and bound in Canada by Metropole Litho

Acknowledgements

Permission to reprint copyright material is gratefully acknowledged. Every reasonable effort to trace the copyright holders of materials appearing in this book has been made. Information that will enable the publisher to rectify any error or omission will be welcomed.

"Pop Bottles" by Spike Milligan, From *Pop Bottles* copyright © 1987 by Ken Roberts; "Eels" by Spike Milligan from "FOR LAUGHING OUT LOUD," Alfred A. Knopf, 1991; "Adventures of Isabel" by Ogden Nash from "MANY LONG YEARS" by Ogden Nash. Copyright 1936 by Ogden Nash, copyright © renewed; "The Duck" by Ogden Nash. *First appeared in THE SATURDAY EVENING POST by permission of Little, Brown and Company; "Nicholas tickle us" by Sol Mandlsohn. From the book "Nicholas tickle us" by Sol Mandlsohn; "Thunder and Lightning" by *Anonymous* from "FOR LAUGHING OUT LOUD," Alfred A. Knopf, 1991; "The Latest Case of Ace McTrace," "Ouch Mountain," and "The Many-Tone Phone" by Mick Burrs. Mick Burrs lives and writes in Yorkton, Saskatchewan. So far, at least 600 of his poems have been printed or broadcast. He also writes songs and stories; "Nine Mice" by Jack Prelutsky from "FOR LAUGHING OUT LOUD," Alfred A. Knopf, 1991; "Bugs" by Will Stokes from "THE MOON IS SHINING BRIGHT AS DAY," HarperCollins; "Stringbean Small" by Jack Prelutsky. Text "Stringbean Small" from "THE NEW KID ON THE BLOCK" by Jack Prelutsky. Greenwillow Books, a division of William Morrow & Company, Inc.

Illustrators

The authors and publishers gratefully acknowledge the contributions of the following illustrators: Peter Coates, Sean Dawdy, Susanna Denti, Daniel Dumont, Norman Eyolfson, Franklin Hammond, Kim LaFave, Stephen MacEachern, Allan Moon, Jun Park, Dusan Petricic, Alain Reno, Bill Suddick

Photographs
p. 84 – © 92 Bryan F. Peterson / Masterfile
p. 88 – © 93 Jose L. Pelaez / Masterfile
p. 92 – © David W. Hamilton / The Image Bank
p. 100 – © 93 Tom and Deeann McCarthy / Masterfile

Reviewers
The authors and publishers gratefully acknowledge the contributions of the following educators:

Halina Bartley
Peterborough, Ontario

Jackie Copp
Winnipeg, Manitoba

Kim Kovacs
Winnipeg, Manitoba

Dr. Georgina Hedges
St. John's, Newfoundland

Adrienne Hopper
Coldbrook, Nova Scotia

Joanne LeBlanc-Haley
Fredericton, New Brunswick

Michele Miller
Fort McMurray, Alberta

Robert M. Rayner
St. Stephen, New Brunswick

Lori Rog
Regina, Saskatchewan

Janice Stone
Ajax, Ontario

3 4 5 ML 00 99 98

Table of Contents

Lesson		Page

About Your Nelson Spelling Book

Here are the features in your spelling book that will help you become a better speller.

Spelling Patterns

4   -er, -or

Each **Lesson** looks at a spelling pattern. A poem, short prose piece, or picture will show you some words that have the spelling pattern.

Your Lesson Words

In each lesson you will use the **Word Box** to make a list of **Lesson Words** with the pattern you will be learning to spell. Sometimes we will include a few **challenge words** that we often find difficult to spell. You will be keeping your own **Personal Dictionary List** of words to use during your own reading, writing, and spelling.

WORD BOX

actor
tractor
editor
monitor
winner
leader
officer
pitcher
daughter
trailer

Zoom in on Your Words

AT HOME

Activities, puzzles, and games will help you learn the meaning and spelling of words. You will practise your Lesson Words and learn new words. **TRY THIS!** announces an extra challenge you may want to try. You will be doing an activity at home. Sometimes you will be asking someone at home to help you.

Spelling Strategies

STRATEGY SPOT — Highlight Word Parts

You can use a special way to highlight a part of a word to remember the spelling. For example, drawing a "ghost" shape around a silent letter reminds you that the sound is "invisible" to the ear.

Grammar

Focus on Language ▶ Commas

Focus on Language gives you information and activities on English grammar. You can use these activities during writing time.

Connecting with ... Other Subjects

Here you will find activities that help you use spelling strategies in reading, writing, and completing projects in other school subjects.

A Focus on Your Own Reading and Writing

Connecting with Literature activities and the poems and short prose pieces included throughout your book will let you study words in authentic reading situations.

SPELL CHECK Every sixth lesson is a review of the spelling patterns and strategies you have been learning. You will be using the Lesson Words you still need to practise in games, puzzles, and other activities.

Quick Tips will give you useful information and tips about patterns and meanings of words. You can use these tips right away in the lesson!

DID YOU KNOW? will tell you interesting information about how our language grew and how it works.

FLASHBACK

What is a good way to remind yourself to say all of the sounds in a word?

Flashback is a quiet time at the end of each lesson to think over what you have learned.

Spelling Stretch is a special section of exciting games and challenges in the back of this book. Find out more about words and make your spelling skills stretch.

Spelling **S T R E T C H**

Have fun reading this silly poem.

Recipe for Poison Shmoison

Take dried snake in a coil,
Two teaspoons of toad oil,
Mix in trouble and some toil,
Add an apple that's really spoiled.

Bring quickly to a bubbling boil,
Cover with a tent of foil,
Add a pinch of old worm soil,
Put in the oven till nicely broiled!

— Kennedy Logan

Creating Your Word List

WORD BOX

choice
moist
boil
noise
soil
poison
join
pointed
coins
voice
spoil
broil

Say these words:

choice   moist   noisy   soil

What sound do these words have in common? Which 2 letters produce the sound? The pattern **oi** is called a **diphthong**. In a diphthong, 2 vowels combine to make a new sound.

1. As a class, make a list of words that have the **oi sound**. Use the poem to help you. As you read each word in the list out loud, really STRESS the **oi sound**.

2. Work with your teacher to create the list of **oi** words you will be learning to spell.
You can use: the Word Box, the poem, your own words. These are your Lesson Words.

3. In your notebook
   • Write the Lesson Words and underline the **oi sound**.

- A Personal Dictionary will help in your reading and writing. You may want to add some of these **oi** words to your Personal Dictionary List.

Give It a Go! — Leave a Blank

When you are writing and are not sure how to spell a word, spell as much of it as you can. For example, if you are not sure how to spell moist, you might spell it like this: m ___ st. Come back to the word later, ask a friend for help, or check the dictionary, your Lesson Words, or your Personal Dictionary List.

Have a partner dictate your Lesson Words to you. If you are not sure how to spell the whole word, draw a line for the missing letters. Correct your words.

Zoom in on Your Words

1. **Wordprints** A footprint shows the shape of a foot. A **wordprint** shows the shape of a word. Draw the shape of each of your Lesson Words. For example:

boil   choice

2. **Out and In** Put the small words back inside the bigger words to make Word Box words.

a) mo __ __ t   **b)** co __ __ s   **c)** poi __ __ __
d) cho __ __ __   **e)** br __ __ __   **f)** jo __ __

3. **Chosen Explosion** Watch the word **choose** "explode"!

choice
choosing

choose

chooses   chose
chosen

Explode the words below. Write as many new words as you can. Use a dictionary to check each word.
a) point   **b)** boil   **c)** poison

TRY THIS! For an extra challenge, pick 3 of the new words and use them in interesting sentences.

choice
chosen

QUICK TIP

When you are exploding a root word, sometimes the spelling changes. For example: choose, choice, chosen.

4. Be Choosy! Choose the correct form of the word **choose** to complete each sentence in your notebook. Read out loud to make sure your choices **sound** correct.

a) My mother gave me a _____ .

b) I could _____ between going to the movies with my friends or going for pizza with the family.

c) I _____ going to the movies.

d) Sometimes I have a hard time_____ the best thing to do.

e) Have you ever _____ the wrong thing?

5. Circle It! Write your Lesson Words and use a coloured pencil to circle any part of a word that gives you problems. Like this:

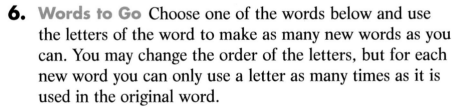

choi(ce)   s(oi)l

AT HOME

6. Words to Go Choose one of the words below and use the letters of the word to make as many new words as you can. You may change the order of the letters, but for each new word you can only use a letter as many times as it is used in the original word.

a) poisoned   b) pointer   c) broil

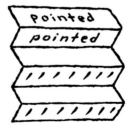

7. Foldover Fold a piece of paper like a fan. Make 6 folds. Print a Lesson Word you want to practise on the first fold. Fold over so you can't see the word. On the next fold write the word again. Open up the paper and check your spelling. Repeat practising your word on each fold. Be sure to check for the correct spelling each time you write the word.

FLASHBACK

How would you describe yourself as a speller? What are 2 things you would like to learn this year about spelling?

Labelling Diagrams

Labelling diagrams clearly and neatly will help you keep your notes organized. Diagrams give information in a simple form. In the example below, the words are printed, lines are drawn with a ruler, and words are printed horizontally.

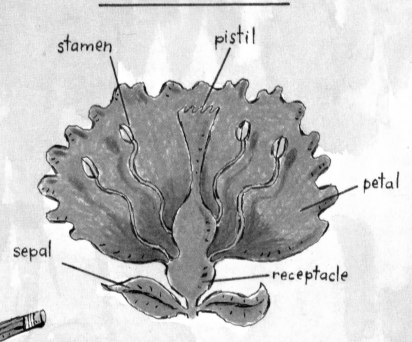

Parts of a Flower

Before you complete the activity below, practise by tracing your hand and labelling all the parts.

1. Find a science topic you are learning now. Draw a detailed diagram about the topic. Label it clearly and completely.

2. Add a title to your diagram.

3. **Proofread** to check the spelling of your labels.

4. Use your spelling strategies to spell words that you need more help remembering.

Enjoy these goofy knock-knock jokes.

Knock, knock.
— Who's there?
Annie.
— Annie who?
Annie one for pizza tonight?

Knock, knock.
— Who's there?
Don.
— Don who?
Don you know?
You're looking right at me!

Knock, knock.
— Who's there?
Betty.
— Betty who?
Betty can't talk as fast as I can!

Knock, knock.
— Who's there?
Robin.
— Robin who?
Robin is wrong!
Let's pay instead.

Creating Your Word List

WORD BOX

chalkboard
doubt
stalk
writer
limb
although
wrong
wrestle
know
brought
February
scissors

Say these words:

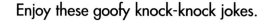

writer   know   limb   brought

What is the same in these 4 words? All of the words have **silent consonants**.

1. As a class, make a list of words that have **silent consonants**. Use the knock-knock jokes to help you. Put the words into a chart like this:

silent consonant at the beginning	silent consonant in the middle	silent consonant at the end

2. Work with your teacher to create the list of **silent consonant** Lesson Words you will be learning to spell. You can use: the Word Box, the jokes, your own words.

12

3. In your notebook

- Write the Lesson Words. Circle the **silent consonants**.
- Keep adding **silent consonant** words to your Personal Dictionary List. Keep it up to date to help in your reading and writing.
- Read the knock-knock jokes with a partner.

  TRY THIS! For an extra challenge, pick 3 of the new words and use them in interesting sentences.

STRATEGY SPOT

Highlight Word Parts

w rong

You can use a special way to highlight a part of a word to remember the spelling. For example, drawing a "ghost" shape around a silent letter reminds you that the sound is "invisible" to the ear.

Zoom in on Your Words

1. **Missing Letters** Help! The computer is about to crash! It keeps missing letters. Fill in the missing letters in your notebook to write Word Box words.

   a) _ _ iter   **b)** dou _ _   **c)** ch _ _ kboard
   d) _ im _   **e)** _ _ ong   **f)** _ _ issors

2. **Disappearing Letters** Make your own missing letter puzzle for 6 of your Lesson Words. Copy down the words and leave a blank for each **silent consonant**. Have a partner fill in the missing silent letters.

3. **Waist and Waste** **Homophones** are words that sound the same but are spelled differently and have different meanings. Here is an example of a pair of homophones:

   I put a belt around my **waist.**   Don't **waste** paper.

   Write down the homophone pairs and draw a little picture beside each homophone. Start a class list of homophones.

AT HOME

4. **Shhh! I Can't Hear You** Make a list of 20 things that are silent in your home. (Bonus points for each of the words on your list that have **silent letters!**)

5. Word Sort Sort your Lesson Words into this chart.

Silent Consonants						
w	k	h	b	l	r	gh

TRY THIS! For an extra challenge, find at least one more word for each **silent consonant** heading on the chart.

6. Is That a or an? Use each of these words in a short sentence. Put **a** or **an** before each word:
a) half   b) ghost   c) hour
d) wrestler   e) honour   f) human

7. All Sorts Write each Lesson Word on a separate small piece of paper. Sort your words in different ways: Sort by number of letters, sort by alphabetical order, sort by **noun**, sort by **verb**, sort by **adjective**. Tell how you sorted the words to a partner.

8. Word Pole Copy and complete this Word Pole. Use the clues to write Word Box words. When you are done, the word in the pole will tell what an author does.

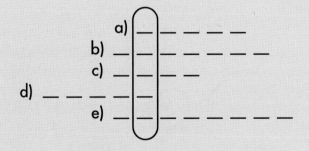

a) opposite of **right**
b) what a wrestler does
c) your leg is one
d) not sure
e) follows January

9. Word Chain See how long a Word Chain you can make. Write down a Lesson Word. Use the last letter of that word to start the next word. Like this:

coins   soil   limb

Use other words you know to continue the chain.

an animal

QUICK TIP

A or **an**? Use **an** before a word that starts with a **vowel** or a **silent h**. For example: **a** limb, **an** animal, **an** honest person.

Focus on Language ▶ Commas

Use **commas** (**,**) to separate 2 or more **adjectives** (describing words) that come before a **noun**. For example:

We live in a small, friendly neighbourhood.

1. Copy these sentences into your notebook and add any missing commas.
- **a)** The hairy scary green monster chased me home!
- **b)** We got a big happy dog at the Humane Society.
- **c)** I ate a juicy hot dog and a small crunchy salad for lunch.

2. Find 3 **adjectives** to describe each of these nouns. Write a sentence for each noun. Watch those commas!
a) wrestler   **b)** writer   **c)** chalkboard

TRY THIS! Stretch your list! Working with a partner, combine the adjectives you used for your sentences and write new, longer (and more descriptive) sentences.

FLASHBACK

What are some letters or patterns that make English tricky to spell? What is a good way to remember how to spell tricky word parts?

Read this newspaper article about some unlucky thieves.

DUFTOWN — Two would-be thieves entered Self Serve grocery, wearing scarves to hide their faces. One unlucky thief bumped into a shelf of knives. A knife flew into the bakery shelves, hit the bread loaves, and a loaf landed on the thief's face, knocking off his disguise. The fleeing bandits were caught when the store manager recognized the not-too-bright scarfless thief as a recent applicant for a job at Self Serve.

Creating Your Word List

WORD BOX

thief
thieves
knife
knives
life
lives
loaf
loaves
scarf
scarves
self

Say these words:

thief   *thieves*   *knife*   *knives*

What happens to the words ending in **-f** and **-fe** when they are made **plural** (to mean more than one)? Notice how the **-f/-fe** ending changes to **-ves** when the singular word is made plural.

1. Make a list of words that end in -f, -fe/-ves. Use the news story to help you. Put the words into a chart like this:

-f to **-ves**	**-fe** to **-ves**

2. Work with your teacher to create the list of -f, -fe/-ves Lesson Words you will be learning to spell.
You can use: the Word Box, the article, your own words.
Include this challenge word in your Lesson Words:

chief

Challenge words are words that most people find difficult to spell.

3. In your notebook

- Write each Lesson Word and <u>underline</u> the part that you need to practise.
- Add new **-f, -fe/-ves** words that you find in your reading and writing to your Personal Dictionary List.

TRY THIS! Write a headline for the news story.

Zoom in on Your Words

1. A, B, C Write your Lesson Words in alphabetical order.

2. In Your Hand Use your finger to "print" each Lesson Word in the palm of your hand.

3. One or More **Singular** means "one" and **plural** means "more than one." Write a sentence with both the singular and plural form of 1 of your Lesson Words. For example:

All **thieves** know that you can never trust a **thief**.

Do the same for 3 more Lesson Words.

4. Looking for Clues Look to other words in a sentence to help you figure out if words are plural or singular.

<u>Porcupines</u> **have** many sharp quills.

Have is the clue that lets you know that the word **porcupine** is plural. First, copy each sentence in your notebook and add the correct form of the missing Word Box word. Second, <u>underline</u> the word that tells you if the missing word should be plural or singular.

a) My _____ is too dull to cut this cardboard.

b) The _____ dropped their stolen goods.

QUICK *TIP*

The word **chief** is an exception to the **-f** to **-ves** pattern.

5. **Dictionary Hunt** Print your Lesson Words on single slips of paper. Before you start, turn the words face down. Now turn 1 word face up. As the word is turned over, players find the dictionary page where the Lesson Word is printed. Do the same with each of the other words.

TRY THIS! For an extra challenge, choose 3 words you would like to learn to spell and find them in the dictionary.

6. **Disappearing Letters** Print your Lesson Words and leave blanks for some of the letters. Like this:

th _ _ f

Now have a partner go back and fill in the missing letters.

7. **Do It Yourself** Write the missing **-self** or **-selves** words to complete these sentences in your notebook. For example: I read my notes to **myself**.

    a) Read it for _____ if you don't believe me.
    b) She can do it _____ now that she is five.
    c) He completed the work all by _____ .
    d) We were proud of _____ for finishing the race.

DID YOU KNOW?

Dictionaries usually give the **plurals** of words. Check the dictionary for unusual plurals, such as: pitch**es**, berr**ies**, ox**en**.

AT HOME

8. **Better Letters** Choose 3 of your Lesson Words and print them in fancy and colourful letters. If you have a computer at home, you may want to use it to design your letters.

FLASHBACK

What is a good way to remind yourself to say all of the sounds in a word?

Pop Bottles

"They're all bottles," said Ray, surprised.

"Pop bottles," corrected Will.

"They aren't chipped or anything, are they?"

"I can see right down inside one of them. It's fine."

"Then they're a treasure," Ray said breathlessly.

"Right." "What's a treasure?" asked a deep voice. Ray stood up. He and Will slowly turned around.

"Hi, creeps."

— from *Pop Bottles*
by Ken Roberts

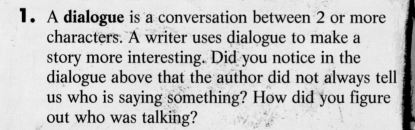

1. A **dialogue** is a conversation between 2 or more characters. A writer uses dialogue to make a story more interesting. Did you notice in the dialogue above that the author did not always tell us who is saying something? How did you figure out who was talking?

2. The author kept the story going without having to say who was talking each time someone said something.
   a) Who asked, "They aren't chipped or anything, are they?"
   b) Who said, "Right"?
   c) Why does the author not always say who is speaking?
   d) What were the other words the author used instead of **said**?
   e) In a small group, brainstorm a list of at least 5 words a writer could use instead of **said**.

19

Can you guess the subject of this poem?

Sleek black shadows, drifting, sniffing, seeping in and out of the trees. Watchers who lurk — waiting with eyes of yellow, burning embers.
Running in packs of primal power. Fear to those who must be predator and prey.
When the harsh blanket of night falls over their sacred ground, you can hear the haunted sounds from the highest mountain peaks, echoing into the lowest of valleys — letting all creatures know that they are the rulers and the spirit of the north woods.

— Amanda Emme, age 13

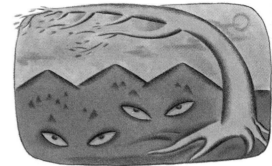

Creating Your Word List

WORD BOX

actor
tractor
editor
monitor
winner
leader
officer
pitcher
daughter
trailer
announcer
quarter

Say these words:

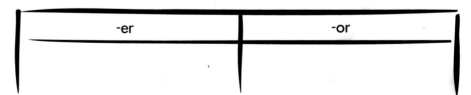

winner   leader   editor   tractor

What sound do these 4 words share? Can you hear the sound of **"er"** in these words? What 2 endings make this sound?

1. Make a list of words that end in **-er** and **-or**. The poem will help you. Put the words into a chart like this:

-er	-or

2. Work with your teacher to create the list of **-er** and **-or** words you will be learning to spell.
You can use: the Word Box, the poem, your own words. These are your Lesson Words.

3. In your notebook
- Write each Lesson Word and <u>underline</u> the letters that make the "**er**" sound.
- You may want to add some of these **-er** and **-or** words to your Personal Dictionary List.

TRY THIS! The poem at the beginning of this lesson is called "**Wolves**." Can you think of another good title for the poem, without telling what the subject is?

STRATEGY SPOT

Exaggerate It!

Some words contain letters and sounds that we usually do not pronounce. To remember their spelling, pronounce the words in an exaggerated way. Saying and hearing these letters will help you remember the correct spelling.

1. Say these words, exaggerating the highlighted sounds:

pit**c**her, ar**c**tic, Feb**r**uary

2. Brainstorm a list of words that have letters or sounds you do not normally pronounce.

Zoom in on Your Words

winn**er**

1. Circle It Write the Lesson Words that have the **-er** pattern. Circle **-er** in each word.

TRY THIS! For an extra challenge, "print" the word in a partner's hand and have him or her guess the word.

2. Picture It Make a clear picture in your mind of each of the **-er** words. Imagine the **-er** in a bright colour.

3. Highlight the Sound Write each of the **-or** words. Highlight the letters you will exaggerate. Now say each word to a partner and have her or him spell the word.

DID YOU KNOW?

These 10 words make up one-fourth of all the words we read: **the, and, of, that, in, to, a, I, it, is.**

4. **Silent TV** List the names of 10 TV shows that have silent letters. Put a ghost shape around the silent letters.

5. **What Do You Do?** We can add **-er** to some words to make the names of occupations (what people do). Like this:

write — A writ**er** is a person who writes.

Make new words by adding **-er**. Write the new words in your notebook.
a) office b) pitch c) lead
d) manage e) consume f) announce

TRY THIS! For an extra challenge, make a list of 6 other jobs that end in **-er** or **-or**.

6. **Who Does It Belong To?** We use an **apostrophe** (') to show that something belongs to someone:

That is my brother**'s** bike.

Use each word in a sentence, showing that something belongs to it.
a) actor b) trailer c) pitcher

7. **This to That** Use the Word Box to figure out these matching **word pairs**. Write the completed sentences in your notebook.
a) **Father** is to **son** as **mother** is to _____ .
b) **Loser** is to _____ as **sad** is to **happy**.
c) _____ is to **batter** as **forward** is to **goalie**.
d) **Farmer** is to _____ as **sailor** is to **ship**.

TRY THIS! For an extra challenge, work with a partner to figure out these pairs. The answers are **-er** and **-or** words.
e) _____ is to **follower** as **engine** is to **caboose**.
f) **Horse** is to **buggy** as **car** is to _____ .

QUICK TIP

The **"er"** sound can also be spelled **ir** or **ur**. These patterns are usually found in the **middle** of words.

FLASHBACK

What is a good way to remind yourself to use your Personal Dictionary during story writing?

Social Studies

Canadian Words

In Newfoundland, a growler is a small iceberg. In Nova Scotia, a fungy is a foggy day. These are words that originated in Canada.

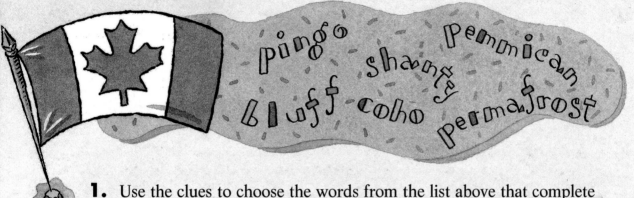

pingo · pemmican · bluff · shanty · coho · permafrost

1. Use the clues to choose the words from the list above that complete this Canadian word quiz:

   a) This 4-letter name of a salmon fish was probably named by the Aboriginal people of the West Coast.

   b) In the Prairies, this word that rhymes with tough means "a clump of trees standing on the flat prairie."

   c) This word was created in 1943 to name the permanently frozen ground in Canada's Far North.

   d) The Inuit call this mound of ice covered with soil a pinguq.

   e) The Cree named this food made from dried meat and melted fat. It comes from their words pimii ("grease") and kan ("prepared").

   f) This word comes from the French Canadian chantier, and is a small, roughly built hut used by lumberjacks in the bush.

2. Use your spelling strategies to spell these Canadian words.

3. Do some research to find other words that are unique to YOUR part of Canada. A librarian will be able to help you. You may also want to ask people in your community.

Would you want to try what the girl in this poem did?

Eels

Eileen Carroll
Had a barrel
Filled with writhing eels
And just for fun
She swallowed one:
Now she knows how it feels.

— Spike Milligan

Creating Your Word List

WORD BOX

allow
attic
happen
battle
recess
worry
borrow
hurry
million
correct

1. Make a list of words that have **double letters**. The poem will help you. Put the words into a chart like this:

double vowels	double consonants – middle	double consonants – end

2. Work with your teacher to create the list of words with **double consonants** you will be learning to spell.
You can use: the Word Box, the poem, your own words. Include these 2 words in your Lesson Words:

horror, stubborn

These 2 words are challenge words.

3. In your notebook
- Write each Lesson Word and highlight the parts you find difficult to spell.
- Add your Lesson Words to the **double letters** chart.
- Keep adding **double consonant** words to your Personal Dictionary List. Don't forget to keep it up to date.
  TRY THIS! For an extra challenge, add 5 more **double letter** words of your own to the chart.

Breaking a word into syllables lets you hear the sounds in the word and gives you information for spelling. Each syllable must have a vowel: rib - bon.

Say your Lesson Words slowly. Write each word and use a coloured hyphen (-) to show how to divide it into syllables.

TRY THIS! Check in your dictionary to see if you have divided the words correctly.

Zoom in on Your Words

QUICK TIP

Double **consonants** in the **middle** of words are always split: at • tack. Double **vowels** usually stay together: look • ing.

1. **Say and Find** Say each of the words on your double letter chart. Underline the **double letter** pattern.

2. **Getting in Shape** Draw the **wordprint** shape of each of your Lesson Words.

3. **Sound Advice** Say each of the words slowly. Listen for the following sound patterns:
   a) Double **vowels**, such as the **e**'s in **eels**, always make ONE **long sound**.
   b) Double **consonants** in the **middle** of words, like the **r**'s in ba**rr**el, usually make TWO sounds: ba**r** - **r**el.
   c) Double **consonants** at the **end** of words, such as the **s**'s in prince**ss**, usually make ONE sound.

Review each of your Lesson Words. If the word follows the general rules for this sound/letter pattern, put a small check mark beside it.

4. **Gone Missing!** That silly computer is skipping letters again! Fill in the missing **double letters** in your notebook.
   a) z _ _   **b)** pi _ _ a   **c)** ri _ _ le
   d) fu _ _ y   **e)** gi _ _ le   **f)** ji _ _ le

   TRY THIS! For an extra challenge, make your own missing letter puzzle for some of your Lesson Words. Have a partner fill it in.

5. Syllable Strips Print your longest Lesson Word on a narrow strip of paper. Fold the paper like an accordion so each fold contains one **syllable**.

6. Correct! It's good news when you hear the word "**Correct**!" Complete each of these sentences in your notebook:

    a) The teacher says "Correct!" when …
    b) I worry about …
    c) I am in a hurry when …
    d) I would like to borrow …
    e) I wonder what would happen if …

TRY THIS! For an extra challenge, draw 3 word balloons with encouraging words or phrases.

7. Spelling Tic-Tac-Toe Each person must use a different-coloured pencil. Player A prints a Lesson Word in 1 square on a tic-tac-toe board. Player B then prints a Lesson Word on the same tic-tac-toe board. Keep adding words until a player has 3 words in a row.

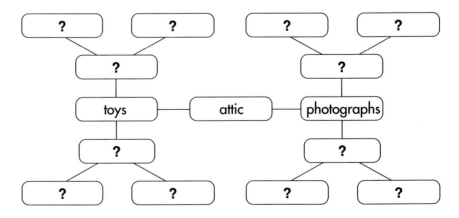

8. That Word Reminds Me of … Say the word **attic**. What 2 other words come to mind? Copy this Word Web in your notebook and complete it using your own words.

Focus on Language ▶ Hyphens

When you are writing a sentence and you run out of space, you can divide the last word on the line into **syllables**. Use a **hyphen** (-) to show that you have divided the word into syllables:

The guide at the park told us that bears like to be by them-
selves in the woods.

1. Copy these words into your notebook and use a hyphen to show where you would divide each word if it came at the end of a line.

a) pitcher   **b)** itself   **c)** mistake
d) eastern   **e)** borrow   **f)** horror

TRY THIS! For an extra challenge, choose 3 of the words and use them in interesting sentences. Break each sentence into 2 lines right after the hyphen.

DID YOU KNOW?

Hyphens are also used to:
- join some **compound words: great-aunt, half-baked**
- join the compound numbers **twenty-one** to **ninety-nine**

AT HOME

2. Syllable Hunt
Write the names of 10 items in your bedroom. Count the number of **syllables** in each word. Rewrite 4 of the words, using coloured **hyphens** to break them into syllables.

FLASHBACK

How does your knowledge of syllables help with spelling?

Creating Your Word List

In your notebook
- Go to your list of "Words I Still Need to Practise."
- Pick 12 words you need to practise spelling. These are your Review Lesson Words.

Zoom in on Your Words

1. **Say It Slowly** S...l...o...w...l...y say each word to yourself and listen to every sound in the word.

2. **Trace It!** Trace over each word with your pencil. Softly say each letter as you trace it.

3. **Focus on It!** <u>Underline</u> the letters you need to focus on. Draw a "ghost" outline around the **silent consonants**. Like this:

4. **v, c, or s?** Is it the **vowels** or **consonants** you are not spelling correctly? Beside each word, write **v** for **vowel**, **c** for each letter you need help remembering.

5. **Unfold the Word** Make Syllable Strips for your longer Review Lesson Words. Practise the spelling as you unfold the strips. See Number 8 on page 26 of Lesson 5 for directions.

6. **Wanted: Silent Consonants!** Copy these words in your notebook, filling in the missing **silent consonants**.
   a) clim _   b) _ res _ le   c) _ nives
   d) attac _   e) _ riter   f) althou _ _

7. **Add-a-Letter** Add a letter to **oil** to make a word that means:
  a) dirt   **b)** a ring   **c)** to work hard
  d) to heat until bubbling   **e)** a thin metal food wrap

8. **Either Or** Add either **er** or **or** to complete these words:
  a) edit _ _   **b)** daught _ _   **c)** moth _ _   **d)** tract _ _
  e) act _ _   **f)** east _ _ n   **g)** winn _ _   **h)** janit _ _

9. **Strategy Review** Look back at the Strategy Spots you have been studying in the last 5 lessons.

10. **Word Stairs** Write down a Lesson Word or other word you can spell. Your partner uses the last letter of the word to start the next word. Do it like this:

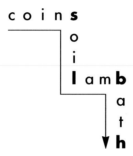

11. **"Let's Talk!"** Rewrite the conversation as a **dialogue**. Be sure to add **quotation marks** and correct **punctuation**.

FLASHBACK

Have a partner dictate your 12 Review Lesson Words. Correct any words you spelled incorrectly. Cross off your list the words you spelled correctly.

Read this poem to find out what happened to an unusual girl.

Adventures of Isabel

Isabel met an enormous bear;
Isabel, Isabel, didn't care.
The bear was hungry, the bear was ravenous,
The bear's big mouth was cruel and cavernous.
The bear said, Isabel, glad to meet you,
How do, Isabel, now I'll eat you!
Isabel, Isabel, didn't worry;
Isabel didn't scream or scurry.
She washed her hands and straightened her hair up,
Then Isabel quietly ate the bear up.

— Ogden Nash

The poem contains words ending in the **suffix -ous**. A **suffix** is a group of letters added to the end of a word to make a new word.

Creating Your Word List

WORD BOX

dangerous
famous
mysterious
mischievous
courageous
enormous
monstrous
adventurous
poisonous
wonderful

1. The **suffix -ous** means "having" or "full of."
Say the new word created when the **suffix -ous** is added to:

danger, courage, fame, mystery

2. The **suffix -ful** can mean "full of" or "enough to fill."
Say the new word created when the **suffix -ful** is added to:

power, cup, delight, wonder

3. As a class, make a list of words that use the **suffix -ous** and words that use the **suffix -ful**.
Read the words out loud and pay attention to the **sound** of **-ous** and **-ful**. Note the changes in spelling when suffixes are added to some words.

4. Work with your teacher to create the list of **-ous** and **-ful** words you will be learning to spell.

You can use: the Word Box, the poem, your own words. Add these 2 words to your Lesson Words:

beauty, beautiful

These 2 words are challenge words.

5. **In your notebook**
- Write each Lesson Word and <u>underline</u> the **suffixes -ous** and **-ful**.
- Add **-ous** and **-ful** words to your Personal Dictionary List to help in your reading and writing.

Zoom in on Your Words

1. **Break It Up!** Write all of your Lesson Words, using a coloured **hyphen** to break up the syllables. Like this:

e - nor - mous

2. **Alphaspell** Write your Lesson Words in alphabetical order.

STRATEGY SPOT

Study Your Spelling Words

Here are 5 great ways to study your spelling words.

1. "Print" the letters with your finger on your palm. Say the letters as you "print."

2. Make a missing letter puzzle. For example, to focus on **double letters** you could do: **mi _ _ ing, le _ _ er.**

3. Close your eyes and visualize the word in your mind. Open your eyes, write the word, and check to see that you have spelled it correctly.

4. Highlight the parts of the word you need help remembering. As you practise, exaggerate the pronunciation of these letters.

5. Print the word on a strip of paper. Fold the paper like an accordion so each fold contains 1 **syllable**. Spell the word aloud as you unfold each syllable.

Do you have your own special spelling strategies? Share them with a partner.

3. Presto Chango! The suffixes **-ous** and **-ful** turn **nouns** (naming words) into **adjectives** (describing words). Write the **noun** and **adjective** forms of each of your Lesson Words and complete this chart in your notebook.

noun	adjective
monster	monstrous

QUICK TIP

We change the final **y** to **i** before adding **-ous** and **-ful**. We usually drop the final **e** before adding **-ous** (fam**e** – fam**ous**).

TRY THIS! Use 3 of the adjectives in sentences.

4. Which Is Right? Choose the word that is correctly spelled in each row and write it in your notebook.
  a) fameous, famous, famious, femous
  b) monsterous, monsterious, monstrous, monstrus
  c) enormus, enorimous, enoormous, enormous
  d) dangerous, dangeros, danjerous, dangirous
  e) mysteryous, mysterous, mysterious, misterious
  f) beautyful, beutiful, beautyfull, beautiful

5. Crossword Time Find your Lesson Words and write them in your notebook.

Across
1 very pretty
4 opposite of **cowardly**
5 mountain climbing is this
6 not well-behaved

Down
2 huge, gigantic
3 superstars are this

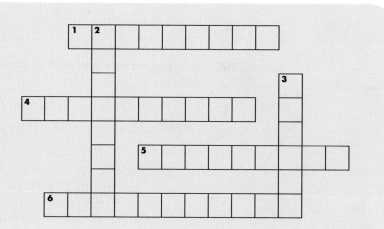

6. Mystery Word Print a Lesson Word on a card. Use a second card to cover all the letters except the first. Ask a partner to guess the hidden word. Move the card to show one more letter at a time until your partner guesses the word.

7. **A Famous Word Web** Copy and complete this Word Web in your notebook.

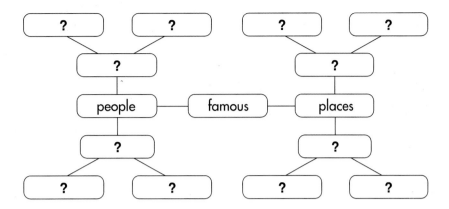

Focus on Language ▶ Proper Nouns

The name of a particular person, place, building, event and date, or thing is called a **proper noun**. **Capital letters** are used to begin proper nouns:

Laura **S**ecord, **R**abbi **F**reeman, **B**art **S**impson
Canada, **H**udson **B**ay, **S**addledome, **R**obson **S**treet
Second **W**orld **W**ar, **M**iddle **A**ges, **T**uesday, **J**une

Find the **proper nouns** in these sentences and rewrite them using correct capitalization.

   a) The actor visited disney world in orlando, florida.
   b) We went on vacation to the rocky mountains.
   c) In may, we visited the alberta provincial museum.

TRY THIS! For an extra challenge, write a list of 10 places in your province and town or city that are **proper nouns**.

FLASHBACK

Which spelling strategy helped you the most to study your spelling words in this lesson?

Here's a poem you might like to share with a young child.

Nicholas tickle us

Nicholas tickle us, make us all laugh,
"I will if you pay me a dime."
Too dear, Nicholas, cut that in half,
Just a nickel, a tickle a time.

— Sol Mandlsohn

Creating Your Word List

WORD BOX

bicycle
gentle
popsicle
simple
whistle
trouble
nickel
novel
shovel
cancel
parcel
signal

Say these words:

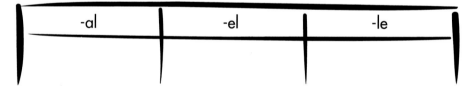

nickel   tickle   signal

Can you hear the sound of **"el"** in these words? Did you notice that the endings sound the same but are spelled differently?

1. Make a list of words that have the **"el" sound**. Use the poem to help you. Put the words into a chart like this:

-al	-el	-le

2. Work with your teacher to create the list of words that have the **"el" sound** you will be learning to spell. You can use: the Word Box, the poem, your own words. These are your Lesson Words.

3. In your notebook
- Write each Lesson Word and circle the letters that make the **sound** of "el."
- Keep adding new **-al**, **-el**, and **-le** words to your Personal Dictionary List.

Does It Look Right?

When you are not sure how to spell a word, write it 2 different ways. Then circle the way that looks right. For example, which word looks right: simple, or simpel?

Try this strategy with some of your Lesson Words. Write each word 2 different ways. Have a partner circle the word that looks right in each pair. Check the words.

Zoom in on Your Words

1. Wordprint Match Match each of the **wordprints** with one of your Lesson Words:

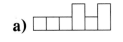 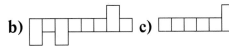

 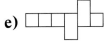 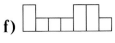

a)   b)   c)

d)   e)   f)

2. Easy/Hard Find 2 or more words that are **synonyms** (same meaning) of each of these Lesson Words:
a) simple   **b)** gentle   **c)** trouble

TRY THIS! Use 1 pair of synonyms in the SAME sentence.

3. Word Search Find the **-al**, **-el**, and **-le** words in the puzzle and write them in your notebook.

u	s	a	d	y	i	s	g	h	s
l	h	x	x	m	i	a	e	f	p
i	o	r	b	g	e	l	l	s	u
t	v	x	n	l	c	e	i	a	z
t	e	a	t	i	c	e	r	u	z
l	l	s	s	n	l	r	z	n	l
e	a	p	a	k	i	t	o	r	e
c	o	c	c	v	e	v	k	p	l
p	w	a	a	z	e	x	z	t	j
z	t	l	l	l	k	u	e	n	e

4. **Disappearing Letters** Print your Lesson Words and leave blanks for some of the letters. Like this: gent _ _ . Now have a partner go back and fill in the missing letters.

5. **Double Jeopardy** Pick a Lesson Word and write clues to describe it. For example: This is 5 cents. Answer: What is a **nickel**? Read your clues to a partner and see if she or he can guess your Lesson Word. Do this with 3 more Lesson Words.

6. **Double Your Fun** One scoop of ice cream is a **single**, two scoops make a **double**. Find out the number words that describe these servings of ice cream:

DID YOU KNOW ?

When books first began to be printed in the 1400s, printers sometimes made mistakes. Some of these mistakes have ended up as our modern-day spellings. For example: someone confused the word **rime** with the word **rhythm**, so now we spell it **rhyme**. The sharp tool called **an awl** was originally **a nawl**. A printer put the space in the wrong place.

AT HOME

7. **Tackle These Sentences** Copy down each of the sentence beginnings below. Complete the sentences at home. Read them to someone.
   a) It is simple to …
   b) They got in trouble when …
   c) Just signal if you …
   d) I was amazed that the huge parcel …

FLASHBACK

Complete each sentence: As a writer, I can … As a writer, I want to …

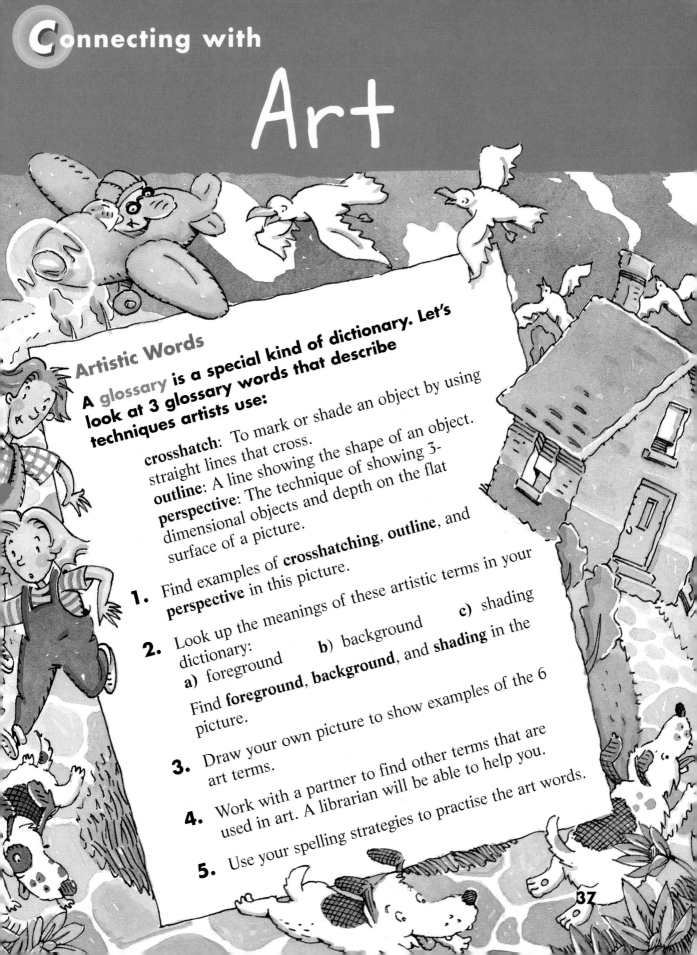

Connecting with Art

Artistic Words

A **glossary** is a special kind of dictionary. Let's look at 3 glossary words that describe techniques artists use:

crosshatch: To mark or shade an object by using straight lines that cross.

outline: A line showing the shape of an object.

perspective: The technique of showing 3-dimensional objects and depth on the flat surface of a picture.

1. Find examples of **crosshatching**, **outline**, and **perspective** in this picture.

2. Look up the meanings of these artistic terms in your dictionary:
   a) foreground b) background c) shading

   Find **foreground**, **background**, and **shading** in the picture.

3. Draw your own picture to show examples of the 6 art terms.

4. Work with a partner to find other terms that are used in art. A librarian will be able to help you.

5. Use your spelling strategies to practise the art words.

What sort of newspaper stories might go with these headlines?

Creating Your Word List

WORD BOX

sigh
flight
slight
flashlight
bright
mighty
fighting
tighten
nightly
lightning
delightful
highlight

Say these words:

high   night   flight   tighten

What **long vowel sound** do these words share? What 2-letter pattern makes the **long i sound** in these words? What other ways can you spell the **long i sound**?

1. Make a list of words that have the spelling patterns **igh** and **ight**. Use the headlines above to help you. As you read each word in the list out loud, really STRESS the **long i sound**.

2. Work with your teacher to create the list of **igh** and **ight** Lesson Words you will be learning to spell.
You can use: the Word Box, the headlines, your own words.

3. In your notebook
- Write each Lesson Word and underline each part of the word that gives you problems.
- Be sure to keep your Personal Dictionary List up to date.

TRY THIS! Pick 1 of the headlines above and draw a picture to describe it. Use the art techniques from page 37.

Look for Word Origins

Many English words come from other languages. Finding out where a word comes from can help you to remember it and understand how it is related to other words you know. Some dictionaries give word origin information. For example, flight comes from the Old English word flyht, which means "to flee."

QUICK TIP

To help you remember the **silent consonants** in **igh/ight** words, draw a "ghost" shape around them.

Zoom in on Your Words

1. **Word Family Tree** Look at the many word branches that can be made from the word **light**:

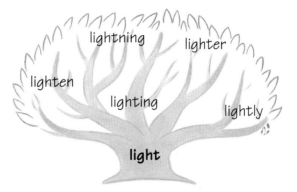

lightning   lighter   lighten   lighting   lightly   **light**

Grow a word tree for each word below. Write as many new words as you can. Use a dictionary to check your words.
a) fright   **b)** tight   **c)** sight
TRY THIS! Use 3 of the new words in sentences.

2. **A Mighty Word Pole** Copy and complete this Word Pole. The word will tell what a spooky tale gives you.

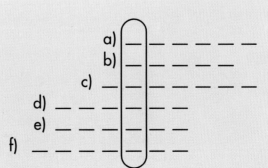

a) comes from the word **fly**
b) opposite of **wrong**
c) how often you sleep
d) a _____ light
e) powerful
f) fix a loose screw

3. Draw What Happened Draw a cartoon strip to tell the highlight of your school day.

4. Hink-Pink A riddle with a rhyming pair of words as the answer is a **hink-pink**. For example: What do you call a crowded airplane trip? A **tight flight**. Use **igh/ight** words to write hink-pink answers to these riddles.

What do you call:
    a) a scary bright flash during a thunderstorm?
    b) being able to see in the dark?
    c) doing something right 2 times?
    d) a smart lamp?
    e) a little battle?

TRY THIS! For an extra challenge, make up your own hink-pinks to share with a partner.

DID YOU KNOW ?

Our words **light** and **fright** come from the Old High German words **lioht** and **forhta** ("fear"). **Sight** and **mighty** come from the Old English **gesiht** and **mihtig**.

---

5. Bright Adjectives Find all the **adjectives** in the headlines at the top of page 38. Now complete these sentences in your notebook:
    a) On a bright, hot day, I …
    b) The beast gave a mighty roar and …
    c) An amazing sight met our eyes when …
    d) With a frightening moan, the …

TRY THIS! For an extra challenge, rewrite 2 of your sentences, adding even more descriptive adjectives. Remember to **proofread** your work.

6. Concentration Cut a sheet of paper into 20 equal-sized squares. Write 10 Lesson Words twice — 1 word per square. Number the **back** of the squares from 1 to 20. Lay the squares down so the numbers are showing. Take turns turning over any 2 numbers until you get a pair of matching words.

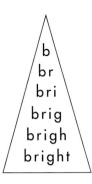

b
br
bri
brig
brigh
bright

7. Word Pyramid Choose a Lesson Word that you need to practise. Draw a triangle in your notebook. On the first line, print the first letter of the word. On the second line, print the first 2 letters. On the third line, the first 3 letters. Continue until the triangle is full. Build a word pyramid with 2 other Lesson Words.

Focus on Language ▶ Adjectives and Adverbs

We can describe an apple as a **small**, **juicy**, **sweet**, **red** fruit. Words like **small**, **juicy**, **sweet**, and **red** are **adjectives**.

1. Copy and complete these sentences, using **adjectives**:
  a) The _____ , _____ athlete jumped over the _____ , _____ highjump bar.
  b) The _____ , _____ wheelchair racer won the race.
  c) The _____ , _____ swimmer dived into the _____ , _____ water.

We can describe **how**, **when**, or **where** an action happens. We can say: The snake **quickly** (how?) slithered **here** (where?) **later** (when?). Words like **quickly**, **here**, and **later** are **adverbs**.

2. Rewrite these sentences and add descriptive **adverbs**:
  a) The horse galloped. (**how?**)
  b) The bison herd stampeded. (**when?**)
  c) Their cat climbed. (**where?**)

3. Complete each sentence in your notebook using both **adjectives** AND **adverbs**:
  a) The _____ , _____ lizard jumped _____ .
  b) The _____ , _____ crocodile swam _____ .
  c) A _____ , _____ frog leaped _____ _____ .

FLASHBACK

When you have an At Home spelling activity, where do you do it? (At the kitchen table? In front of the TV?) When do you do it? Who can you ask for help?

Let's look at two definitions from the dictionary. Notice all the things the dictionary tells about each word:

communicate (kə myū′ nə kāt′) *v.* to tell something to others by talking, writing, or using technology: *We will communicate by e-mail later.* **communicating. communicated.**

create (krē āt′) *v.* **1.** to make something new: *The inventor created a new kind of skate.* **2.** to cause: *The fan's fast rate of spin created a rattling of plates.* **creating. created.**

Creating Your Word List

WORD BOX

plate
slated
later
rate
create
relate
chocolate
grateful
skaters
date
gateway
communicate

Say these words:

late   create   gateway

What **long vowel sound** do these words have? What letter pattern makes the **long a sound** in these words? What other spelling patterns have the **long a sound**?

1. Make a list of words that have the spelling pattern **ate**. Use the definitions above to help you. As you read each word in the list out loud, really STRESS the **sound** of **ate**.

2. Work with your teacher to create the list of **ate** words you will be learning to spell.
   You can use: the Word Box, the definitions, your own words.
   These are your Lesson Words.

3. **In your notebook**
   • Write each Lesson Word and underline the **ate** pattern.
   • You may want to add some of these **ate** words to your Personal Dictionary List to help in reading and writing.

Zoom in on Your Words

1. Wordprints Draw the **wordprint** shape of each of your Lesson Words. "Feel" the shape the **ate** pattern makes.

2. Checkup! Have a partner dictate your Lesson Words.
- Write down each word as your partner reads it out loud.
- Check your words and correct any spelling mistakes.
- ★ Put a star beside the words you need to review.

3. Create a Break Write each of your Lesson Words, using coloured hyphens (-) to break the words into syllables.

STRATEGY
SPOT

Create Word Stories

You can make up a story to help you remember the spelling of a tricky word. It can be a simple phrase: a **friend** in the **end**. These memory helpers are called mnemonic devices.

4. At a Mighty Rate Draw a line down the centre of a page in your notebook. Write **ight** at the top of 1 column, and **ate** at the top of the other column. In 3 minutes, write as many words as you can that contain these patterns. Score 1 point for each correctly spelled word. Lose 1 point for any spelling that is not a real word. Have fun!
> TRY THIS! Use 3 of your words in interesting sentences.

5. Magic Endings Be a word magician! In your notebook, write the root words you can pull out of the first hat. Then add a different ending to make a new word for the second hat.

Root Words

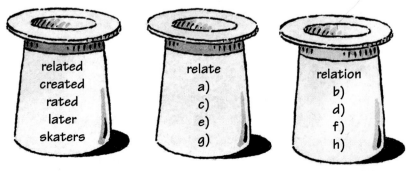

Hat 1:
related
created
rated
later
skaters

Hat 2:
relate
a)
c)
e)
g)

Hat 3:
relation
b)
d)
f)
h)

6. Chocolate Dreams Write a list of 12 chocolate things. You'll get lots of practice spelling the word **chocolate**, and you'll get to dream of fun things to eat.

7. Communication Web Copy this Word Web in your notebook and complete it using your own words.

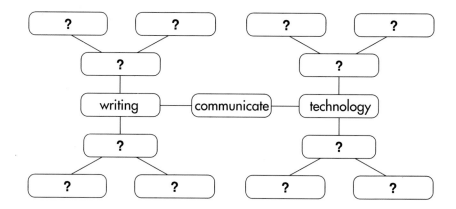

QUICK TIP

Most **ate** words have the **long a sound**. **Chocolate** is an exception. Check in the dictionary if you are not sure how to **pronounce** a word.

DID YOU KNOW?
Mnemosyne is the name of an ancient Greek mythological being called a Titan. She was associated with memory.

8. Don't Be Late! Copy the sentences into your notebook and use the correct form of **late** for each missing word.
   a) _____ , I've had trouble getting up in the morning.
   b) This means I am often _____ for school.
   c) Each day, I'm arriving _____ and _____ .
   d) Now I'm the _____ student in the whole school.

9. Word Stories Use the spelling strategy to write a word story for 1 Lesson Word. To get started, think:
   • What little words can I see in the word?
   • What little words can I hear in the word?
   • What special ideas are connected with the word?

10. Memory Game Play this game in a group. Player A says "I went on a trip and took a … (something that begins with **a**)." Player B says "I went on a trip and took a … (repeats the **a** item) and a … (adds something that begins with **b**)." Keep taking turns repeating all the items and adding a new one. Can you make it to **z**?

Focus on Language ▶ Dictionary Pronunciations

After each word in the dictionary, you will find the word written again (in brackets) using **phonetic symbols** (sim′ bəlz). Different dictionaries may use different symbols, but the **pronunciation** is the same. This **pronunciation key** helps you in 3 ways by showing: how to pronounce the word, how many syllables it has, and which syllables to stress when you say the word.

1. Find 3 words in the dictionary that you don't know how to say. Use the **pronunciation key** to help you say each word.

2. Look up the words below in your dictionary. In your notebook, divide each word into syllables and write the number of syllables it has. Mark the syllables you stress.

    a) grateful   **b)** communicate   **c)** relation

Vowel Sounds

a	as in **a**nd, b**a**d, s**a**ng		i	as in **i**f, s**i**t, w**i**ll
ā	as in f**a**ce, **a**ble, m**ai**l		ī	as in **I**, f**i**ne, b**y**
à	as in **a**rt, c**a**r, h**ea**rt		o	as in **o**n, p**o**t, p**aw**
e	as in b**e**nd, h**ea**d, wh**e**n		ō	as in r**o**pe, s**oa**p, **ow**n
ē	as in b**e**, b**ee**, **ea**t		ò	as in **o**rder, ab**oa**rd, c**o**re
ə	as in met**a**l, brok**e**n, penc**i**l, bac**o**n, circ**u**s		u	as in **u**p, **o**ther, s**u**ng
	(ə is an unstressed vowel called a **schwa**)		ū	as in r**u**de, c**oo**l, bl**ew**, sh**oe**
			ù	as in f**u**ll, c**oo**k, f**u**r, s**ea**rch

---

3. Use the above **pronunciation guide** and choose the phonetic spelling that matches each meaning:

    a) a large body of fresh water   līk   lak   lāk
    b) connects your body to your head   nik   nok   nek
    c) you can ride this   bāk   bīk   bik

FLASHBACK

Look through this book and find 2 or 3 spelling strategies you can use when story writing.

Enjoy these verses from "The Walrus and the Carpenter."

The eldest Oyster looked at him
But never a word he said:
The eldest Oyster winked his eye,
And shook his heavy head —
Meaning to say he did not choose
To leave the oyster-bed.

But four young oysters hurried up,
All eager for the treat:
Their coats were brushed, their faces washed,
Their shoes were clean and neat —
And this was odd, because, you know,
They hadn't any feet.

— Lewis Carroll

Creating Your Word List

WORD BOX

agree
reason
either
valley
genie
steal
season
teaching
beneath

Say these words:

me   agree   steal   received

What sound do these 4 words share?

1. Make a list of words that have the **long e sound**. Use the poem to help you. Put the words into a chart like this:

e	ea	ee	ey	ie	ei

2. Work with your teacher to create the list of **long e** words you will be learning to spell.

You can use: the Word Box, the verses, your own words. Add these 3 words to your Lesson Words:

because, received, their

These 3 words are **challenge words**.

3. In your notebook
- Write each Lesson Word and circle the letters that make the **long e sound**.
- Keep adding new **long e** words to your Personal Dictionary List.

TRY THIS! Look in the library for the book *Through the Looking Glass* by Lewis Carroll. Find the poem "The Walrus and the Carpenter" in it. Read the whole poem and add the **long e** words in it to the chart you started.

STRATEGY SPOT   Make an Acrostic

An **acrostic** is a word pattern that helps you remember. For example:

BECAUSE	
	Baby
	Elephants
	Can
	Always
	Use
	Smaller
	Ears.

Making up an acrostic and memorizing it helps you remember all of the letters in a word. Here is how you do it:

1. Print the word you want to spell in a column, from top to bottom.

2. Write a word for each letter. It helps if the words almost make a sentence.

3. Pick a Lesson Word that is challenging for you and try out this spelling strategy.

4. Read a partner's acrostic.

Zoom in on Your Words

1. **Lineup** Write your Lesson Words in order from shortest to longest.

2. Either Or Look in the Quick Tip for the 2 ways to pronounce the word **either**. Survey 6 people by showing them the written word **either** and asking them to say it. Make a chart to record your results:

ei = long e	ei = long i

3. I Stand for ... Make an **acrostic** using the letters in your first and last names.

4. Complete It! Write the completed sentences in your notebook, filling in the missing letters in the Lesson Words:
    a) They can go _ _ ther today or next week.
    b) Tell them a good r _ _ son why they should go now.
    c) Do you agr _ _ with th _ _ r decision to go today?

    TRY THIS! For an extra challenge, copy these sentence beginnings and complete each sentence in your notebook.
    d) My favourite s _ _ son is _____ because ...
    e) Four r _ _ sons t _ _ ching is an important job are ...

5. That Stands for ... An **acronym** is a word made up of the first letters of a group of words. For example: **scuba** = self-**c**ontained **u**nderwater **b**reathing **a**pparatus.
Find the meaning of these acronyms in the dictionary. Write the words each acronym stands for.
    a) radar   **b)** sonar   **c)** laser   **d)** NASA

6. Homophones The words **steal** and **steel** are **homophones**. **Steal** means to take without paying and **steel** is a type of hard metal. **Their** and **there** are also homophones.
Use the correct homophone to complete these sentences:
    a) Is it right to _____ if you have no money to eat?
    b) _____ is made from iron and carbon.
    c) They want you to come to _____ party.
    d) I will meet you over _____ .

7. Agree or Disagree Write a sentence that uses **agree** and **disagree**. For example: I **agree** that hockey is great, but I **disagree** that it is better than baseball.

QUICK TIP

This rule will help you spell **ie** and **ei** words: **i** before **e** when it sounds like **ē** except after **c**. The word **either** is an exception. The **ei** can have the sound of **long e** or **long i**. When in doubt, check in a dictionary.

Focus on Language ▶ Prefixes and Suffixes

A **prefix** is a little word part that we add before a **root word**. A **suffix** is a word part we add at the end.

Prefixes and suffixes are "transformers." They can change a word into its opposite (happy/**un**happy, agree/**dis**agree) or a **verb** into a **noun** (excite/excite**ment**). Nouns can also be changed into adjectives and adverbs (nation/nation**al**/nation**ally**).

prefixes:
il-
un-
dis-
re-
inter-

suffixes:
-ly
-less
-ness
-able
-ity
-ment
-al

1. Add prefixes and suffixes from the box to the following root words. Make as many new words as you can. Check in the dictionary to make sure all the words make sense.
   a) nation   **b)** agree   **c)** like   **d)** hope

2. Now, complete these sentences in your notebook, adding some of the words you have made. The root words after each sentence give you a clue.
   a) Helena's work as an artist is _____ known. (**nation**)
   b) It is _____ that anyone would try to copy one of her paintings. (**like**)
   c) Most countries of the world have signed an _____ _____ that protects an artist's work from being copied. (**nation, agree**)

FLASHBACK

To identify **long e**, you need to **listen** to the sound and **look** at the pattern of the letters. How can you remind yourself to use both senses?

SPELL CHECK

Creating Your Word List

In your notebook
- Go to your list of "Words I Still Need to Practise."
- Pick 12 words you need to practise spelling. These are your Review Lesson Words.

Zoom in on Your Words

1. **Piece by Piece** Slowly say each word to yourself, syllable by syllable. Listen to the sound each syllable makes.

2. **Wordprints** Draw the **wordprint** shape of each word. "Feel" the shape of the letters as you draw.

3. **A, B, C** Write your words in alphabetical order.

4. **A Capital Problem** Amanda is writing a report, but the shift key on her computer is stuck. Help find the **proper nouns** that need **capital letters**. Rewrite the paragraph in your notebook.

> rock climbing is an exciting new sport for many girls my age. to get ready for our july trip, my friends yolanda, meghan, and i went to the kinsmen sports centre to try the climbing wall. although it's not as good as the rockies, it is close to the real thing and you don't even have to leave edmonton.

5. **Word Race** Have a word race with a partner. Write **-le** on 1 piece of paper and **-ous** on another. Each partner has a sheet of paper and in 3 minutes writes as many words as possible that contain these letter patterns. Score 1 point for each correctly spelled word.

6. Agree to Explode! Make **agree** "explode" by adding as many **prefixes** and **suffixes** as you can. Check in the dictionary.

7. Long e Search Go on a **long e** word search throughout the classroom. Think of other **long e** words in your school. To make your search easier, write a chart of the different ways **long e** can be spelled.

8. I'm Thinking of ... Pick a Lesson Word. Give your partner a clue about the word. (Be careful not to say the word!) See if your partner can guess the word in 3 tries.

9. Acrostic Time Write an **acrostic** for 3 Review Lesson Words you want to remember. See page 47 for full directions.

10. Word Chain See how long a word chain you can make. Write down a Review Lesson Word. Use the last letter of that word to start the next word. Like this:

Use other words you know how to spell to continue the chain.

11. Practise Your Spelling Words Look back at the Strategy Spot on page 31 of Lesson 7. Use some of the ideas to study your Review Lesson Words.

12. Adventure Titles Make up titles for 5 adventure stories. Make them so colourful and exciting that all your friends will want to read them. Use your spelling strategies to study any words that you want to practise. Don't forget to **proofread**!

FLASHBACK

Look at the Review Lesson Words you now know how to spell. Cross them off your list of "Words I Still Need to Practise." Your spelling vocabulary is growing every day!

What pictures do you see in your mind as you read this poem?

Thunder and Lightning

The thunder crashed,
The lightning flashed
And all the world was shaken;
The little pig
Curled up his tail
And ran to save his bacon.

— *Anonymous*

WORD BOX

taken
brighten
broken
spoken
golden
stolen
wooden
happened
sharpened
sweetened
women
dozen

Creating Your Word List

1. Say the new word created when **-en** is added to the end:

bright, wood, take

The ending **-en** can be a **suffix** that means "to cause to be" or "made of." Words ending in **e** drop the **e** before adding **-en**.

2. As a class, make a list of words that end in **-en**. The poem will help you.
As you read each word out loud, pay attention to the **sound** of **-en**.

3. Work with your teacher to create the list of **-en** words you will be learning to spell.
You can use: the Word Box, the poem, your own words. These are your Lesson Words.

4. In your notebook
- Write each Lesson Word and underline the **-en**.
- You may want to add **-en** words to your Personal Dictionary List to help in your reading and writing.

 TRY THIS! The words in this poem gave you an image in your mind. Draw a picture of what you saw as you read this poem.

See It — Visualize Words

When you visualize a word, you "see" in your mind what the word looks like.

1. Look at these words: **broken**, **stolen**, **golden**.

2. Close your eyes and get a picture of each word in your mind.

3. Making a picture can help you spell a word. Visualizing the shape of a word can help you spell it.

Zoom in on Your Words

1. **Slow Down!** Slowly say each Lesson Word and listen to every sound. **Visualize** each word as you say it.

2. **Stolen Letters** The letter thief has struck again! Find the missing letters and write the Lesson Words.
   a) st _ l _ n
   b) doz _ _
   c) happ _ n _ d
   d) g _ _ den
   e) sp _ k _ _
   f) t _ k _ n
   g) sharp _ n _ d
   h) b _ _ ken
   i) s _ _ ete _ ed

3. **Scrambled Words** These Lesson Words were scrambled on the computer screen. Write them correctly.
   a) dowone
   b) neglod
   c) dpapnehe
   d) engirhbt
   e) owmne
   f) neatk
   g) wesentdee
   h) rebnok
   i) zedno

   TRY THIS! For an extra challenge, make up your own scrambled word puzzles. Ask a partner to solve them.

4. **Rhyme Time** Choose 1 -en Lesson Word. Write as many words as you can that rhyme. Rhyming words do not have to have the same spelling pattern (tak**en** – bac**on**).

5. **Word Pairs** **Day** and **night** are **word pairs**. Find the missing -en word and write each word pair in your notebook.
   a) **men** and _____
   b) _____ and **written**
   c) **given** and _____
   d) _____ and **darken**

QUICK TIP

When you hear the sound "**en**" at the end of a word, it is usually spelled en. Words that tell that something is being done (sharp**en**, tak**en**) or is made of something (gold**en**, wood**en**) usually end in **-en**.

6. Wooden Word Pole Copy and complete this Word Pole. Use the clues to write **-en** words. When you are done, the word in the pole will tell what a light does.

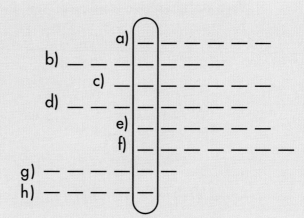

a) if it needs fixing it is ...
b) fix a dull knife
c) make something lighter
d) scare someone
e) to take place
f) fix a loose screw
g) to make damp
h) 12 eggs

a) _ _ _ _ _ _
b) _ _ _ _ _ _
c) _ _ _ _ _ _
d) _ _ _ _ _ _ _
e) _ _ _ _ _
f) _ _ _ _ _ _
g) _ _ _ _ _ _
h) _ _ _ _ _

DID YOU KNOW?

In ancient Egyptian, picture symbols called **hieroglyphs** or **pictographs** were used to stand for meanings and sounds rather than letters. The characters of modern Chinese are based on **pictographs**.

AT HOME

7. Can You Picture It? Choose a paragraph from a book you are reading. Draw a picture that describes it.

8. Thunder and Lightning Read the poem at the top of page 52 out loud to a partner. Describe what you "saw" in your mind as you read. Have your partner describe to you what she or he imagined. Note how the details of your **visualizations** were the same and were different.

FLASHBACK

When you have a partner activity, do you always work with the same person? Next time, work with someone else. When working with a partner, what are some things to remember to do so the activity goes smoothly?

Social Studies

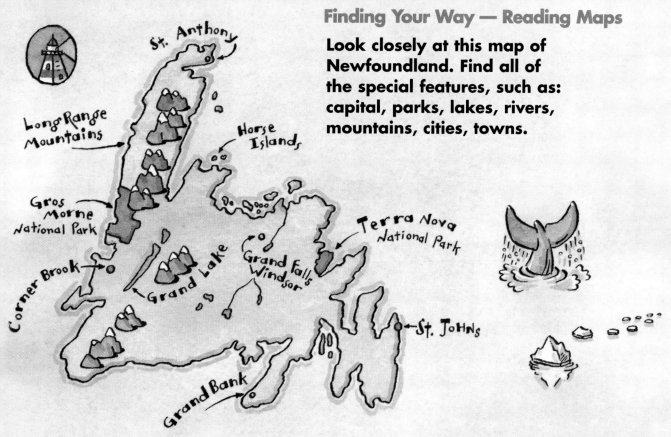

Finding Your Way — Reading Maps

Look closely at this map of Newfoundland. Find all of the special features, such as: capital, parks, lakes, rivers, mountains, cities, towns.

Map labels:
- St. Anthony
- Long Range Mountains
- Horse Islands
- Gros Morne National Park
- Corner Brook
- Grand Lake
- Grand Falls Windsor
- Terra Nova National Park
- St. John's
- Grand Bank

1. Look at a map of your province with a partner.

2. Find the **capital**. How far is it from your town/city to the capital (or another place if you live in the capital)?

3. Find any **rivers**, **lakes**, and **mountains**.

4. Find the **provincial parks**.

5. Can you find any other features on the map?

6. Pick 5 names from the map and use your spelling strategies to learn their spelling. Quietly snap, clap, or tap out the syllables in each name.

7. How did these places get their names? See if you can find out the origins of other interesting or unusual place names on your map.

Enjoy this story about private detective Ace McTrace.

The Latest Case of Ace McTrace

My name is Ace McTrace, Private Eye. You may not believe my latest case, but I'm telling it to you straight. You see, I'm still chasing the guy in the raincoat. He broke into my place last night and stole my rainbow tablecloth. He looked like he just climbed off the nearest spaceship. Five eyes, two heads, no mouth. He escaped into the safety of the foggy night. When he stole that tablecloth, he took my TV dinner with it — plate, silverware, and all! He made a mistake — how's he going to eat it, anyway? Now I'm starving. There must be a better way to make a living!

— Mick Burrs

Creating Your Word List

WORD BOX

fair
rainbow
spaceship
mistake
escape
safety
straight
raincoat
bakery
tablecloth
ache
chasing

Say these words:

fair   escape   mistake

What letter patterns make the **long a sound** in these words? What other spelling patterns have the **long a sound**?

1. Make a list of words that have **long a**. Use the story to help you. Put the words into a chart like this:

ai	a __ e	other

2. Work with your teacher to create the list of **long a** Lesson Words you will be learning to spell.
You can use: the Word Box, the story, your own words.

3. In your notebook
- Write the Lesson Words. Circle the **long a sound**.
- Add **long a** words to your Personal Dictionary List.

Draw Word Pictures

You can use drawings to help you remember the spelling of some words. The drawings should illustrate the meaning or sound of the word. For example:

Rain   Tornado   Fair Weather

Draw 3 Lesson Words in the shape of their **meaning**.

Zoom in on Your Words

1. Long or Short? Sort these words into 2 groups — **long a** and **short a**: tail, wagon, grade, water, apart, break, have, neighbour, rabbit.
★ Put a star beside any words you need to review.

2. Long ABC's Make an alphabet for young children. Write a word with the **long a sound** for each letter of the alphabet. Like this:

$$\textbf{a} – \textbf{a}\text{pe} \qquad \textbf{b} – \text{b}\textbf{a}\text{ke} \qquad \textbf{c} – \text{c}\textbf{a}\text{re}$$

3. All the Same Another word for **ache** is **pain**. Write down a **synonym** (word that means the same or almost the same) for as many Lesson Words as you can.

4. Magic e Adding a **silent e** to the end of a **consonant/vowel/consonant** word changes the **middle vowel sound** from **short** to **long**. For example: răt – rāte
Change these words by adding a final **e**.
a) car   **b)** fad   **c)** bar   **d)** hop

TRY THIS! For an extra challenge, write your own "magic e" word pairs.

QUICK TIP

Here are 3 unusual ways to spell the **long a sound**:
- **ea** like br**ea**k,
- **ei** like n**ei**ghbour,
- **ey** like th**ey**.

5. **Bumblebee** Play the Bumblebee game with a partner. Player A chooses a Lesson Word and writes down a dash for each letter of the word. Player B has to figure out the word by guessing 1 letter at a time. Only 1 guess of the final word is allowed. For every incorrect guess, Player A draws another part of the Bumblebee. Then switch roles. Watch out for that stinger!

聽

DID YOU KNOW?

The Chinese character for the word **listen** is made up of several parts, which include the **ears**, **eyes**, as well as the **heart**.

6. **Different Ways of Sorting** Write each Lesson Word on a small piece of paper. Sort your words in different ways: Sort by meaning, sort by spelling pattern, sort by **vowel sound**, sort by number of letters. Tell how you sorted.

7. **Long a Jeopardy** Pick a Lesson Word and write clues to describe it. For example: This is the very bottom of a house. Answer: What is a **basement**? Read your clues to a partner and see if she or he can guess your Lesson Word.

TRY THIS! Do this with any 4 **long a** words.

8. **Is There Space in a Spaceship?** These **compound words** are based on the word **space**: **spacecraft**, **space suit**, **spaceship**, **space shuttle**.
Write as many compounds as you can for each word below.
a) rain   **b)** air   **c)** table   **d)** fair
Use a dictionary to check the spelling of your new words.

FLASHBACK

Look back at the activities in this lesson. Which activity helped you the most?

The Fox and the Grapes

A hungry fox went all around the countryside, but could not find anything to fill his stomach.

Finally, the beautiful colour of grapes ripening in the sun caught his attention.

Standing under the vine he stared up at the big, juicy bunch of grapes and thought he had finally solved his problem.

He tried to grasp them by reaching up with his paws.

He jumped and jumped and jumped … but he could not get them.

"Just a bunch of sour grapes! Who wants them anyway?" he said to himself as he walked away.

— from *Aesop's Fables* by Fulvio Testa

1. A **fable** is a story with a lesson called a **moral**. Write what you think the moral of this fable is.

2. How could the fox have gotten the grapes?

3. The phrase "sour grapes" is an **idiom**. What do you think it means? Do you know any other idioms?

4. Have you ever felt "sour grapes" about something? Describe the situation to a partner.

5. The adjectives **hungry**, **beautiful**, **juicy**, and **sour** add detail to the story. How do these words help you get a picture in your mind?

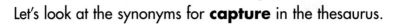

Let's look at the synonyms for **capture** in the thesaurus.

capture   *verb*
• to take something or someone by force. *The cat* ***captured*** *the mouse.*
apprehend   To apprehend means to take someone or something into custody. *The police* ***apprehended*** *the thief when he tried to sell the stolen furniture.*
trap   To trap means to catch something or someone. *They* ***trapped*** *the bully who tore up their pictures.*
hijack   To hijack means to seize something, using threats or violence. *In the adventure story, the terrorists* ***hijacked*** *the plane and forced the pilot to fly to the hidden treasure.*

Find the words that end in **-ure**. You may want to add some of the synonyms to your Personal Dictionary List.

Creating Your Word List

Say these words:

picture   signature   adventure

What sound does **-ure** make? If you were going to spell **-ure** the way it sounds, how would you spell it?

1. Make a list of words that have the **-ure** pattern. Use the thesaurus entries to help you. Read the words out loud and pay attention to the sound of **-ure**.

2. With your teacher create the list of **-ure** words you will be learning to spell.
You can use: the Word Box, the thesaurus entries, your own words. These are your Lesson Words.

WORD BOX

picture
signature
capture
future
furniture
adventure
texture
literature
fracture
feature
moisture
treasure

3. In your notebook
- Write the Lesson Words and <u>underline</u> the **suffix -ure**.
- Keep adding **-ure** words to your Personal Dictionary List. Be sure to keep it up to date.

Find a Word in a Word

To remember the spelling of words, find smaller words in them. For example, the word **sign** is in **signal**. You can also make up little sayings to help you remember the words in words. For example: A **fri**end to the **end**.

Zoom in on Your Words

1. Box and Count Copy your Lesson Words. Draw a box around the **-ure** ending. Quietly snap, clap, or tap out the **syllables**. How many syllables are in each word?

2. Z, Y, X Write your Lesson Words in REVERSE alphabetical order.

DID YOU KNOW ?

Thesaurus comes from the Latin word meaning "treasury" (a place where treasure is kept).

3. Treasure Maze Choose the word parts that make real words when you add **-ture**. Write the new words.

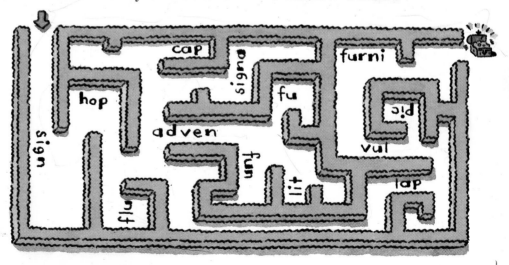

AT HOME

4. Favourite Movie Adventure Write the story of your favourite adventure movie and illustrate the action scene.

5. Noun Hunt Words that end in **-tion** and **-ure** are **nouns**. Find ALL the nouns in these sentences.
   a) I saw a picture of the earth taken from space.
   b) There was no pollution visible in the photograph.
   c) Our planet looked like a beautiful, blue treasure.
   d) It would be a real adventure to go on vacation and explore many parts of the world.
   TRY THIS! For an extra challenge, write down all the **verbs** you can find in the sentences.

6. Hugely Successful **Synonyms** are words that have similar meanings. Write all the words you can think of that are synonyms of **huge**.

7. Finish It! Use words from the Word Box to complete the sentences.
   a) I read a book that is an exciting _____ story.
   b) In it, pirates _____ a boy who has a map to buried _____.
   c) The front of the book has a _____ that shows the route to the treasure.
   d) I liked the book so much that I want to get the author's _____ when she comes to town.
   TRY THIS! For an extra challenge, write a short, interesting paragraph using at least 4 Lesson Words.

8. Texture Web Copy this Word Web in your notebook and complete it using your own words.

QUICK TIP

Can't find a word in the dictionary? Look up a **synonym** you do know how to spell. The definition of the synonym may contain the word you were looking for!

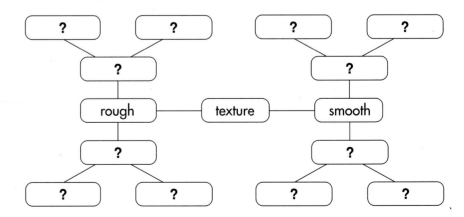

Focus on Language ▶ Thesaurus

A **thesaurus** is a book of words, usually in alphabetical order. Beside each word is a list of **synonyms** (words that have the same meaning). Writers use a thesaurus to find interesting words and expressions.

Some thesauruses also list a few **antonyms** (words with opposite meanings). Here are some sample entries from one kind of thesaurus:

good, considerate, generous, kind, honest, just, agreeable, enjoyable, pleasant, satisfying
antonyms: common, small, average, inferior, selfish

meal, breakfast, brunch, dinner, lunch, supper, mealtime, refreshment, banquet, feast

taste, sample, try, savour, experience, encounter, feel
antonyms: dislike, hate, deplore, detest

The **meal** tasted **good**.

1. This sentence uses ordinary words. Using the sample thesaurus words, rewrite the sentence 3 different ways.

2. Write this sentence once more with the **opposite** meaning.

3. Look over samples of your own writing and choose 3 words that are repeated or are not specific or descriptive enough. Use a **thesaurus** to find more interesting words.

FLASHBACK

When you need help spelling a word, what do you do? What are 3 things you can do to help yourself?

Stand on the bridge and find the **-dge** and **-ge** words in the river.

Creating Your Word List

WORD BOX

badge
bridge
judge
edge
ledge
wage
charge
cage
page

Say these words:

page   budge   charge

What sound do these 3 words share? What letters make the **"j"** sound?

1. Make a list of words with the spelling patterns **-dge** and **-ge**. Use the picture to help you. Put the words into a chart:

-dge	-ge

2. Work with your teacher to create the list of **-dge** and **-ge** Lesson Words you will be learning to spell.
You can use: the Word Box, the picture, your own words.
Include these 3 **challenge words** in your Lesson Words:

it's, that's, you're

Most people find challenge words difficult to spell.

3. In your notebook

- Write the Lesson Words and circle any part of a word that you need help remembering.
- Add **-dge/-ge** words and **challenge words** to your Personal Dictionary List. Keep it up to date.

Proofreading — Read Out Loud

To **proofread** means to check what you have written. When you are proofreading your work, read it out loud softly to yourself. You'll **hear** and **see** your spelling mistakes, missed words, and punctuation problems.

QUICK TIP

-dge or **-ge**? Usually, words that have a **short vowel** right before the "**j**" sound use **-dge** (bri**dge**, le**dge**). Words with a **consonant** before the "**j**" sound use **-ge** (char**ge**, bul**ge**).

Zoom in on Your Words

1. What Do You Hear? What **vowel sounds** do these words have in common?

badge, edge, bridge, lodge, budge

They all have **short vowel sounds**.
Write all your Lesson Words with the **-dge** pattern.
Highlight the **short vowel sound** in each word.

2. What Do You Hear Now? What **vowel sounds** do these words have in common?

wage, siege, oblige, huge

They all have **long vowel sounds**.
Write all your Lesson Words with **long vowel sounds**.
Highlight the **long vowels**.

3. Scrambled Letters Copy this chart in your notebook and unscramble the words that fit under each heading.

-dge	-ge
a) gdbae	b) rhgeca
c) juegd	d) ewag
e) gdbier	f) baergag
g) deeg	h) llivgea

AT HOME

4. **Be A Word Artist!** Pick 5 Lesson Words and draw them in fancy letters that will help you remember their spelling.

5. **Missing Letters** Add the missing letters and write the **-dge/-ge** words in your notebook.
  a) b _ d _ _   **b)** h _ _ e   **c)** j _ _ g _
  d) wa _ _   **e)** br _ _ _ e   **f)** c _ _ rg _
  Add the words to the correct column of the **-dge/-ge** chart.

6. **Word Pole** Copy and complete this Word Pole. Use the clues to write **-dge/-ge** words. When you are done, the word in the pole will tell where ice cubes are kept.

  a) chocolate _____ sundae   a) | _ _ _ _ _
  b) cost for services   b) _ _ _ | _ _ _
  c) crosses a river   c) _ _ | _ _ _ _
  d) _____ and jury   d) _ _ | _ _ _
  e) what someone earns   e) _ _ | _ _
  f) a medal   f) _ _ _ _ |

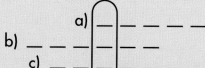
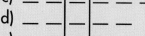

7. **Shortcuts** **Abbreviations** are shortened words. Match these common abbreviations with the full word.
  a) Mt.   Canada
  b) St.   Mister
  c) Can.   mountain
  d) kg   street
  e) Mr.   kilogram

8. **Expand It** Write the complete word(s) for each of these abbreviations:
  a) Dr.   **b)** km   **c)** Ave.   **d)** NS
  e) SK   **f)** U.S.   **g)** Co.   **h)** CBC

Focus on Language ▶ Word Shortcuts — Contractions

A **contraction** is a word shortcut. It is 2 words shortened to 1 word. An **apostrophe** (') shows that 1 or more letters have been left out of a word. Read these contractions and their long forms:

it is	**it's**
she is	**she's**
I have	**I've**
they are	**they're**
he will	**he'll**
will not	**won't**
did not	**didn't**
cannot	**can't**

Write a **contraction** to replace the **bold** words in each sentence.

1. My little sister **cannot** wait to get a pair of inline skates.

2. Last year she **was not** big enough to use them. But now **she is** 8 years old.

3. **I have** told her that she must wear a safety helmet. **It is** just as important to have knee and elbow pads too.

4. A friend of mine had an accident and scraped his forehead. He **did not** wear his helmet. **He had** forgotten to put it on.

5. **I am** going to teach my sister how to skate. **That is** going to be a lot of fun.

6. Some day **she will** be able to teach *me* a trick or two!

FLASHBACK

The best way to remember a new skill is to teach it to someone else. Try teaching your spelling strategies to another student.

Read this jingle. It may be the most famous spelling rule.

i before e except
after c

Like most rules, it has exceptions. But it will help you spell most **ei** and **ie** words.

Creating Your Word List

Say these words:

field   weigh   receive   friend

Do these 4 words follow the "**i** before **e**" rule?

1. Put the words into a chart like this:

ie sounds like "e"	except after c	doesn't sound like "e"	exceptions to rule

2. With your teacher, create the list of **ei** and **ie** Lesson Words. You can use: the Word Box, your own words.
Include these 2 **challenge words** in your Lesson Words:

experience, friend

Add your Lesson Words to the **ei/ie** chart.

3. In your notebook
- Write the Lesson Words and <u>underline</u> the **ei** and **ie**.
- Keep adding **ei** and **ie** words to your Personal Dictionary List. Don't forget to keep it up to date.

QUICK TIP

Science is an exception because the **i** and **e** are in separate **syllables** (sci • ence). **Conscience** is an exception because the **i** gives a "**sh**" sound to the **c**.

Zoom in on Your Words

1. **Count It** Divide your Lesson Words into syllables. Use a coloured pencil to add hyphens (-).

2. **Shape It** Draw the **wordprint** shape for each Lesson Word.

3. **Word Pyramid** Choose a word you want to practise. Draw a triangle in your notebook. On the first line, print the first letter of the word. On the second line, print the first 2 letters. On the third line, the first 3 letters. Continue until the triangle is full. Do a pyramid with 3 other Lesson Words.

4. **Missing Letters** Add the missing letters and write the **ei/ie** words in your notebook.
   a) w _ _ ners
   b) w _ _rd
   c) s _ _ ence
   d) _ _ igh
   e) _ _ ther
   f) fr _ _ n _
   g) f _ el _
   h) hei _ _ t
   i) fi _ _ ce

   TRY THIS! For an extra challenge, use the computer and make your own missing letter puzzle for a partner to solve.

STRATEGY SPOT

Proofreading — Scan Back!

Here's a proofreading tip. Read your work backwards! This way you will pay attention to the spelling of each word instead of the meaning of what you have written. To proofread the sentence: "My friends played soccer in the field," you would read the words in this order: field the in soccer played friends My.

5. **Scan Back!** Help Reiko proofread her writing. Watch out for capital letters, the wrong homophones, and punctuation mistakes!

   I had a wierd experience last weak. eight feild mice ran acrost my kichen floor, One tried to climb into the heighest cuboard? I wanted too captured it to take to sceince class, but it got a weigh. Thay havn't come back sinse;

6. **I Spy...** Choose the correctly spelled word in each line and write it in your notebook.

a)	height	hieght	hight
b)	wiegh	weigh	weaght
c)	freind	friend	frend
d)	sceince	sciense	science

TRY THIS! For an extra challenge, use 3 of the words in interesting sentences. Don't forget to **proofread**!

7. **Cross It Out!** An extra letter has been placed in each of the words below. Write the words and cross out the extra letter in each word by asking yourself "Does this look right?"

a) weirrd **b)** belieive **c)** sciensce

d) eighteeen **e)** fieirce **f)** expeerience

8. **Word Association** Often one word makes us think of another. For example, if you say **sky**, many people will say **blue**. Play Word Association with a partner. Say a Lesson Word and have the person say the first word or words that come to mind. Do this with 4 more Lesson Words.

DID YOU KNOW?

Some common names have a number of different spellings. For example: **Sean, Shaun,** or **Shawn. Megan, Meghan,** or even **Meganne.** When spelling someone's name for the first time, don't rely on your eyes — check with the person!

---

9. **A Weird Reminder** Make a little rhyme or other **mnemonic device** to help you remember the spelling of **weird** (it is an exception to the "**i** before **e**" rule).

AT HOME

10. **Complete the Sentences** Complete each sentence starter at home. Remember to **proofread** your sentences by scanning back!

a) Do you believe that …

b) When I am eighteen, I …

c) It was weird when …

d) Four things I like about science are …

e) A friend is a person who …

Pronouns are "**stand-ins**" for **nouns**. They keep nouns from being overworked.

(noun)   **(pronoun)**

Tina is meeting **her** friends at the movies.

A **subject pronoun** names who or what a sentence is about.

An **object pronoun** is a pronoun that completes the meaning of an **action verb** (**runs**, **went**, **said**) or a form of the verb "**to be**" (**is/am/are**, **was/were**). Here is a chart of common pronouns:

As Subject	As Object
I	me
you	you
he, she, it	him, her, it
we	us
they	them
who	whom

Copy this chart in your notebook. When you are not sure which form of pronoun to use, refer to the chart.

Rewrite these sentences, using the right form of each **pronoun**.

1. Rishan and **me/I** went to the movies last Saturday.

2. **We/Us** fast-food fans love to eat pizza!

3. I gave **she/her** a new pen for **her/she** birthday.

4. It was **I/me who/whom** answered when **them/they** phoned.

FLASHBACK

Challenge words are not spelled the way they sound. What strategies are you using to remember the spelling of **experience** and **friend**?

SPELL CHECK

REVIEW

Patterns

-en
long a
-ure
-dge/-ge
ei, ie

Strategies

1. See it — Visualize words.
2. Draw word pictures.
3. Find a word in a word.
4. Proofreading — Read out loud.
5. Proofreading — Scan Back!

Creating Your Word List

In your notebook
- Go to your list of "Words I Still Need to Practise."
- Pick 12 words you need to practise spelling. These are your Review Lesson Words.

Zoom in on Your Words

1. **Visualize!** Look carefully at each Review Lesson Word. Close your eyes and **visualize** the word in your mind.

2. **Draw It!** Look back at the Strategy Spot on page 57 of Lesson 14. Choose 3 of your words and draw a picture for each word that will help you remember its spelling.

3. **What's the Pattern?** Highlight the letter patterns in each of your Review Lesson Words.

4. **Proofreading Practice** Pick the correct spelling in each row. Then use each word in an interesting sentence. Use the Scan Back! strategy (Lesson 17, page 69) to **proofread** each sentence.
   a) television   telivision   televesion
   b) expect   axpect   ecpect
   c) pitcer   picture   pictire
   d) weiners   wieners   weniers

5. **Stretch It!** Write the full words each **contraction** stands for.
   a) it's   b) that's   c) won't
   d) didn't   e) wouldn't   f) she'll

AT HOME

6. Practise! Look at the Strategy Spot on page 31 of Lesson 7. Use some of the ideas to study your Review Lesson Words.

7. Dictionary Trick

Jesse: But you can't look up a word in the dictionary that you can't spell!

Terra: Try looking up a similar word.

Write a **synonym** Jesse could use to help him find the dictionary spelling of each of the following words.

a) ache   **b)** beneath   **c)** least

8. See the Word Each of these picture puzzles stands for a common phrase. For example:

Man Overboard

Solve these picture puzzles by writing the phrases in your notebook:

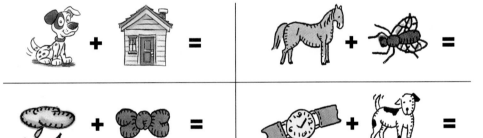

FLASHBACK

Look at the Review Lesson Words you now know how to spell. Cross them off your list of "Words I Still Need to Practise." Bravo! You're becoming a spelling superstar.

Read this tale of nine mice out loud.

Nine Mice

Nine mice on tiny tricycles
went riding on the ice,
they rode in spite of warning signs,
they rode despite advice.

The signs were right, the ice was thin,
in half a trice, the mice fell in,
and from their chins down to their toes,
those mice entirely froze.

Nine mindless mice, who paid the price
are thawing slowly by the ice,
still sitting on their tricycles
... nine white and shiny micicles!

— Jack Prelusky

How did you know how to pronounce the last word?

WORD BOX

slice
reduce
false
force
purse
distance
produce
silence
whose
advice

Creating Your Word List

Say these words:

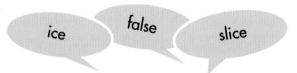

ice   false   slice

What sound do these 3 words have in common? What letters make the "**s**" sound? When **c** is pronounced as "**s**" it is called a **soft c**.

1. Make a list of words that end in **-ce** and **-se**. Use the poem to help you. Put the words into a chart like this:

-ce	-se

Breaking a word into syllables lets us hear the sounds in the word and gives us information for spelling. Let's review:
- **Each syllable must have a vowel:**
- **Double consonants in the middle of words are split:**
- **Double vowels usually stay together:**
- **A vowel can sometimes stand alone in a syllable:**
- **Silent e's stay with their voiced vowels:**

ti • ny
at • tack
look • ing
Is • a • bel
pro • duce

For each guideline above, find any 2 words that follow the guideline. Break them into syllables.

2. Work with your teacher to create the list of **-ce** and **-se** Lesson Words you will be learning to spell.
You can use: the Word Box, the poem, your own words. Include these 2 challenge words in your Lesson Words:

decide, decision

3. In your notebook
- Write the Lesson Words and circle any part of a word that you need help remembering.
- Add **-ce/-se** words and challenge words to your Personal Dictionary List. Keep it up to date.

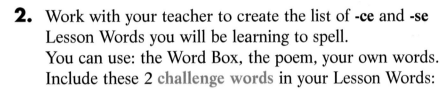

QUICK TIP

Words like advice/advise and practice/practise are spelled with a **c** AND an **s**. The **c** spelling is a **noun**. The **s** spelling is a **verb**.

Zoom in on Your Words

1. c or s? Decide to add a **c** or an **s** and write the completed words in your notebook.
a) de _ ide   **b)** fal _ e   **c)** surpri _ e
d) produ _ e   **e)** sli _ e   **f)** de _ i _ ion
g) distan _ e   **h)** silen _ e   **i)** advi _ e

TRY THIS! Read the Quick Tip. For an extra challenge, write a sentence using **practice** (**noun**) and a sentence using **practise** (**verb**).

AT HOME

2. Scrambled Words The mice knocked over the Word Box! Unscramble the letters and write the words.

a) usper   b) dueecr   c) acdeinst
d) sohwe   e) elicnse   f) ecupdro

3. Crossword Time Find your Lesson Words and write them in your notebook.

Across
4 helpful suggestions
5 a choice
6 synonym of **quiet**

Down
1 true or _____
2 1 of the recycling 3 **r**'s
3 cut into pieces

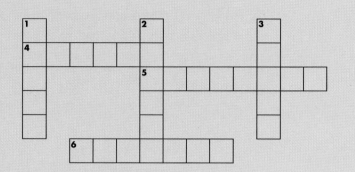

4. From A to Z Sort your Lesson Words in alphabetical order. Compare your answers with a partner.

5. Letter Ladder Write your longest Lesson Word in a column, from top to bottom. Use Lesson Words and other words you can spell to fill the ladder. Do it like this:

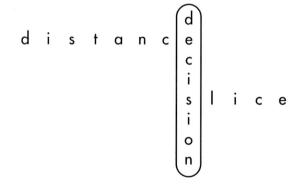

FLASHBACK

What strategy did you use to spell **-ce** and **-se** words?

Sports Dictionary

Most sports have their own vocabulary. For example, baseball has a number of words that are specific to the game. For example: batter, pitcher, catcher, foul ball, outfield, infield, shortstop, base hit, home run. If you were going to make a dictionary just for baseball players, these words would be in it.

Let's make a
SPORTS DICTIONARY!

HERE'S HOW:

1. Pick your favourite sport. With a partner or in a small group, brainstorm at least 10 words used in that sport.

2. Put these words in alphabetical order.

3. Look in a dictionary to help complete the next 3 steps:
   a) Tell whether each word is a **noun**, **verb**, **adjective**, or **adverb**.
   b) Write a short **definition** for each word.
   c) Write a sample sentence to help show the meaning.

4. Choose words that a picture would help describe. Draw pictures or find photos for these words.

5. Remember to use your spelling strategies!

6. Don't forget to **proofread** the final copy of your work.

Have fun reading about this wonder of technology.

The Many-Tone Phone

Oh, the many-tone phone has so many new tones, when it rings you know just who is calling!
When it coughs like someone's bad sore throat, you can bet it's the doctor calling.
When it sounds like a hole tearing open your coat, you know it's the dry cleaner calling.
A ring like crashing bowling pins says you've got the sports store calling.
And when it moans like the ghostly bones of a spooky tale, you're relieved it's the library calling!

— Mick Burrs

Creating Your Word List

WORD BOX

board
bones
toad
tomato
tornado
throat
stove
grown
goal
wore
hero
bowling

Say these words:

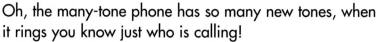

board   bones   throat   bowling

What **vowel sound** do these 4 words have in common?

1. Make a list of words that have the **long o sound**. Use the poem to help you. Put the words into a chart like this:

o __ e	oa	ow	– o	other

2. Work with your teacher to create the list of **long o** words you will be learning to spell.
You can use: the Word Box, the poem, your own words.

3. **In your notebook**
- Write the Lesson Words and <u>underline</u> the **long o sound**.
- You may want to add **long o** words to your Personal Dictionary List to help in your reading and writing.

STRATEGY
SPOT

I Know That Pattern! — Word Families

Word families help you to spell new words. You know how to spell home, **so by following the o __ e pattern you can now spell** stove, wrote, **and** froze.

QUICK *TIP*

Here are 4 unusual ways to spell the **long o sound**: br**oo**ch, s**ew**, plat**eau**, m**au**ve.

Zoom in on Your Words

1. **Say Oh!** Complete these **long o** words in your notebook.

   a) thr _ _ t   **b)** s _ _ ve   **c)** to _ d
   d) b _ n _ s   **e)** t _ m a _ _   **f)** gr _ _ n

2. **Find More** Add 2 words to each column of the chart on page 78.

3. **Change-a-Letter** Change 1 letter in each of these words to make a new word.

   a) toad   **b)** bow   **c)** cone
   d) hole   **e)** post   **f)** store

4. **Pole Words** Copy and complete this Word Pole. Use the clues to write Word Box words. When you are done, the word in the pole will name a violent wind.

   a) an appliance for cooking   a) _ _ _ _ _
   b) a sport with pins and balls   b) _ _ _ _ _ _ _
   c) a piece of lumber   c) _ _ _ _ _
   d) they form a skeleton   d) _ _ _ _ _
   e) in ketchup and salsa   e) _ _ _ _ _
   f) an amphibian animal   f) _ _ _ _
   g) opposite of **young**   g) _ _ _

5. **A Tornado of Words** Use the letters in the word **tornado** to write as many new words as you can. You may use each letter more than once. Write at least 10 words.

6. **Homophones** Words that sound the same but are spelled differently and have different meanings are called **homophones**. Some **long o** words are homophones:

groan – grown, rowed – rode, toad – towed

Write down the 2 words in each homophone pair and draw a small picture to illustrate each one. Add the pairs to your class list of homophones. With a partner, think of at least 3 more **long o** homophone pairs.

7. **Word Trips** Complete this **word trip**. Copy the boxes and follow the arrows to fill in the spaces. Write a word you think of when you say the word in the box you just left.

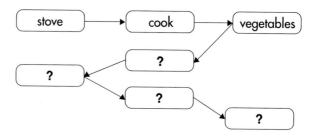

Make 2 of your own word trips. Start with **long o** words and make each word trip at least 7 words long.

8. **Proofread!** Pick the correct spelling in each row. Then use 3 of the words in interesting sentences. Use the Scan Back! strategy on page 69 to proofread each sentence.

a) throte	throwt	throat
b) tomatoe	tomato	tamato
c) windoe	windo	window
d) gowl	goal	gole

FLASHBACK

Design a cue card showing the ways **long o** is spelled and keep it in your desk for easy reference.

Languages

First Languages

Canada's Aboriginal languages are part of our heritage. Here are the pronunciations of the names of the months in Tuscarora (an Iroquoian language):

January	Kaw-wih-kyah	July	Aw-ken-haw-kyah-haw
February	Kaw-nih-dah	August	Aw-ken-haw-kyah-hah-thoo
March	Kaw-neh-haw-rih-kyah	September	Raw-thah-kyah-haw
April	Naw-kaw-hah-rhahd	October	Raw-thah-kyah-hah-thoo
May	Kah-nahs	November	Koo-sah-seh-haw
June	Joo-yow-thaw-kyah	December	Koo-sah-seh-hah-thoo

1. Why do you think the months of July and August begin with the same sound?

2. Use the Tuscarora pronunciations to write the month of:
   a) your birthday
   b) your favourite holiday
   c) your favourite month

3. In a small group, brainstorm a list of things people can do to keep Aboriginal languages alive.

4. Languages carry a lot of information about a people: how they live, what is important to them, how they communicate. Did your ancestors speak a language other than English? Does this effect your family traditions (names of foods, family names, names of holidays)?

DID YOU KNOW ?

Of Canada's 53 Aboriginal languages, 43 may die out before the 21st century. Only 3 — Cree, Ojibwa, Inuktitut — have an excellent chance of surviving. Aboriginal languages may survive because they are being written and taught in schools.

Here's a shorter poem about bigger bugs.

Bugs

Oh, them big bugs have bigger bugs
That jump on 'em an' bite 'em,
An' them bigger bugs have other bugs
An' so ad infinitum.

— Will Stokes

Do you know what **ad infinitum** means?

Creating Your Word List

<table>
<tr><td>

WORD BOX

longer
bigger
biggest
lower
younger
older
shorter
simpler
swifter
milder
tinier
emptier

</td></tr>
</table>

Say these words:

Say the new word created when the **suffixes -er** and **-est** are added to these words:

loud   big   tiny   simple

Notice how the **root word** changes in some words when **-er**, **-est** are added. The **suffixes -er**, **-est** make the **comparative form** of adjectives and adverbs. They let you compare 2 or more things.

1. Make a list of words that end in the **suffixes -er** and **-est**. Put the words into a chart like this:

root word	-er	-est

2. Work with your teacher to create the list of **-er** and **-est** words you will be learning to spell.
You can use: the Word Box, the poem, your own words.

3. In your notebook
- Write the Lesson Words and circle **-er** and **-est**.
- Add **comparison** words to your Personal Dictionary List.
- Have fun rewriting the poem, using your own words to replace the underlined words.

STRATEGY SPOT

Find Related Words — Meaning Patterns

Words that have the same root word are called related words. Words that are related in meaning may not always have similar pronunciations, but they often have similar spelling. For example, watch the root word sign "explode":

signal signature signing   sign   signed significance significant

Say each word and notice what happens to the sound of g.

Zoom in on Your Words

QUICK TIP

Some comparison words have **irregular forms**: good/well, better, best bad, worse, worst much, more, most

1. Make More Add **-er** and **-est** to some of these words. Be careful, not all of the words can have **-er** and **-est**!
- **a)** tall
- **b)** short
- **c)** mild
- **d)** joyful
- **e)** told
- **f)** gentle

2. Change and Add Add **-er** and **-est** to these words.
- **a)** tidy
- **b)** funny
- **c)** tiny
- **d)** sleepy
- **e)** tasty
- **f)** windy

3. More Difficult Words that end in **-ful/-ous/-able/-less** and words with 3 or more **syllables** use **more** and **most** instead of **-er/-est** (**more** careful, **most** careful — **more** difficult, **most** difficult.) Write the **comparison forms** of these words.
- **a)** joyful
- **b)** experienced
- **c)** anxious
- **d)** hopeless
- **e)** able
- **f)** lovable

DID YOU KNOW?

Ad infinitum is a Latin phrase meaning "forever." Its literal translation is "into infinity."

4. **Smart, Smarter, Smartest** Adjectives describe people, places or things. They can be used to compare similar objects. For example:

That bike is **light**.
Mine is **lighter**, but Sarah's is the **lightest**.

Copy and complete this chart. Watch for irregular forms.

adjective	-er	-est
light	lighter	lightest
a) _____	older	**b)** _____
c) swift	**d)** _____	**e)** _____
f) _____	**g)** _____	**h)** youngest

TRY THIS! Using the words from the comparison chart, write 3 interesting sentences. Use at least 2 forms of the same word in EACH sentence.

5. **Compare and Contrast** Complete these phrases in your notebook, adding the missing **-er** adjectives.
   a) not as large as an elephant, but _____ than a horse
   b) not as bad as a broken arm, but _____ than a cut
   c) not as small as a pebble, but _____ than a baseball
   d) not as windy as a tornado, but _____ than a breeze

TRY THIS! Illustrate 2 of the phrases.

AT HOME

6. **Opinion Poll** Interview someone at home. Find out what he or she thinks is **good**, **better**, and **best** for each category.

	good	better	best
books	_____	_____	_____
television shows	_____	_____	_____
songs	_____	_____	_____

FLASHBACK

How has learning about suffixes helped you become a better speller?

Timelines

A timeline shows important events during specific periods of time. The timeline displays a lot of information in a small space. This timeline shows some important events in the history of a school.

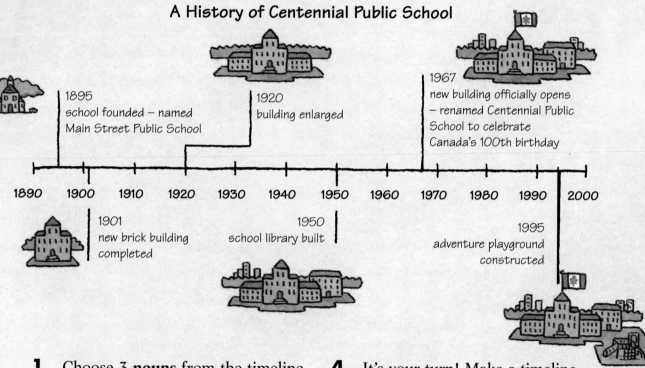

A History of Centennial Public School

1895
school founded – named
Main Street Public School

1920
building enlarged

1967
new building officially opens
– renamed Centennial Public
School to celebrate
Canada's 100th birthday

1890 1900 1910 1920 1930 1940 1950 1960 1970 1980 1990 2000

1901
new brick building
completed

1950
school library built

1995
adventure playground
constructed

1. Choose 3 **nouns** from the timeline and write them in your notebook.

2. Choose 3 **verbs** and write them in your notebook.

3. Pick 3 words you need to work on and use your spelling strategies to learn their spelling. Quietly snap, clap, or tap out the syllables in each name.

4. It's your turn! Make a timeline of your school's history. Use **point-form** (you don't need to start your notes with capital letters or end them with periods). Give your timeline a title. Add pictures to make it more interesting.

5. Use your timeline as the basis for a story about your school's history.

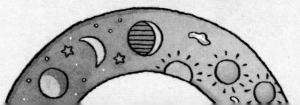

Enjoy this poem.

Ouch Mountain

You can touch Ouch Mountain
with all your fingers.
It's really no bigger than a boulder.

You can lift this mound upon your shoulder,
then toss the big rock high
into the cloudy sky.

When Ouch Mountain falls back to the ground,
you better dodge it, you better crouch,
because, of course, if it hits you — *ouch!*

— Mick Burrs

Creating Your Word List

WORD BOX

cloudy
mountain
amount
tough
youth
mound
dough
shoulder
touch
group
boulder
though

Say these words:

cloud   scout   sound

What sound is made by the **ou** pattern? If you were going to spell **ou** the way it **sounds** in these words, how would you spell it?

Now say these words:

touch   group   dough

What **3** sounds does the **ou** pattern make in these words? If you were going to spell the different sounds **ou** makes in these words, how would you spell them?

1. Make a list of words that have the **ou pattern**. Use the poem to help you. Put the words into a chart like this:

"ow" sound	long o sound	short u sound	long u sound

2. Work with your teacher to create the list of **ou** words you will be learning to spell.
   You can use: the Word Box, the poem, your own words.

3. **In your notebook**
   - Write the Lesson Words and underline **ou**.
   - Add **ou** words to your Personal Dictionary List.

   TRY THIS! For an extra challenge, add at least 2 words of your own to each column in the chart.

STRATEGY
SPOT

Proofreading — Does It Look Right?

When proofreading your work, underline any words that do not look right. Now check your underlined words in a dictionary, in your Personal Dictionary List or ask someone else. When writing, always get your ideas down FIRST and then go back and double-check any spellings you are not sure of.

Zoom in on Your Words

1. **Try Your Eye!** Pick the word that looks right in each row and write it in your notebook.

   a) showlder   sholder   shoulder
   b) amont   amownt   amount
   c) freind   friend   firend
   d) mownten   mountin   mountain

AT HOME

2. **Idioms** Use 3 of these **idioms** in meaningful sentences:
   a) won't get off the ground   b) in the same boat
   c) a shoulder to cry on   d) smell a rat
   e) a mountain out of a mole hill   f) play with fire

3. **Homophones and Homographs** Words that sound the same but are spelled differently and have different meanings are called **homophones**:

foul – fowl, doe – dough

Write down the 2 words in each homophone pair and use each word in a sentence that shows its meaning.

Words that are spelled the same but have different meanings and different pronunciations are called **homographs**:

A **tear** fell from his eye.
Don't **tear** that piece of paper.

Find the homograph pairs below in your dictionary and draw a picture to show the meaning of each word.
a) wind/wind   **b)** present/present   **c)** bow/bow

QUICK TIP

There are many ways to pronounce the **ou pattern**. Check the **pronunciation keys** in your dictionary when you are not sure.

DID YOU KNOW?
Letting the cat out of the bag (giving away a secret) is an idiom. An **idiom** is an expression whose meaning cannot be understood simply from the words used.

4. **Many Meanings** A word can have many meanings. The meanings change according to how we use the word:

The computer **course** starts next week.
The golf **course** was crowded with people.

Write 2 sentences for each of these words. Show a different meaning in each sentence.
a) touch   **b)** ground   **c)** tough   **d)** amount

FLASHBACK

Add a **homophone pair** and a **homograph pair** to your Personal Spelling Dictionary.

Connecting with

Literature

Alice's Adventures in Wonderland

… suddenly a White Rabbit with pink eyes ran close by her. There was nothing very remarkable in that; nor did Alice think it so very much out of the way to hear the Rabbit say to itself, "Oh dear! Oh dear! I shall be too late!" (when she thought it over afterwards, it occurred to her that she ought to have wondered at this, but at the time it all seemed quite natural); but when the Rabbit actually took a watch out of its waistcoat pocket, and looked at it, and then hurried on, Alice started to her feet, for it flashed across her mind that she had never seen a rabbit with either a waistcoat pocket or a watch to take out of it, and burning with curiosity, she ran across the field after it, and was just in time to see it pop down a large rabbit-hole under the hedge. In another moment down went Alice after it, never once considering how in the world she was to get out again.

— from *Alice's Adventures in Wonderland* by Lewis Carroll

1. The author wants the reader to feel the same emotion as Alice. What words describe this emotion?

2. Find the interesting phrases the author uses to say:
   a) thought   **b)** got up
   c) seemed okay   **d)** go in the ground

3. Visualize the story setting in your mind. Draw a picture of what it might look like.

4. Select 1 of your own stories. Read it over and find a place where you can add some details about what is going through a character's mind. Try adding 2 or 3 sentences that describe the character's thoughts.

Some dictionaries have special **usage notes** that help you use words and word parts. Read this usage note about **-ly**.

> **-ly** is a suffix that is added to many adjectives to turn them into adverbs. *It is a quick squirrel. The squirrel climbs quickly.* In these sentences, **quick** is an *adjective* and **quickly** is an *adverb*.

Creating Your Word List

Say these words:

slow   slowly   angry   angrily

What sound is made by the **-ly** ending? Notice what happens to the **y** in angr**y** – angr**i**ly.

1. Make a list of words that end in the **suffix -ly**. The **usage note** above will help you.

2. Work with your teacher to create the list of **-ly** words you will be learning to spell.
You can use: the Word Box, the note, your own words.

3. In your notebook
 • Write the Lesson Words and circle each **suffix -ly**.
 • Add **-ly** words to your Personal Dictionary List.
 TRY THIS! Pick a **prefix** and a **suffix** you want to learn more about and look them up in your dictionary.

Zoom in on Your Words

1. Finding Roots Write your Lesson Words and their **root words**. Like this: **curly – curl**.

WORD BOX

especially
suddenly
bravely
carefully
slowly
lonely
daily
excitedly
quietly
usually
angrily
lightly

2. Oppositely Attracting! Write the Lesson Words that are the opposite of these words:
a) quickly   b) cowardly   c) carelessly
d) slowly   e) noisily   f) heavily

TRY THIS! For an extra challenge, draw small pictures to illustrate 3 Lesson Words and their opposites.

STRATEGY SPOT

Proofreading — Share It!

Sometimes it is difficult to find the spelling and punctuation errors in your own work. Ask a partner to proofread your work with you. By reading aloud together, you'll spot the mistakes a lot faster.

3. Syllable Count The word **com • fort • a • bly** has 4 **syllables**. Count the syllables in your Lesson Words.

4. Word Machine The new-word machine adds the **suffix -ly** to words that go in it. Put these words through the new-word machine:
a) most   b) human   c) noise
d) lucky   e) fearless   f) comfortable

TRY THIS! Use 3 or more of your new words in a short paragraph. **Proofread** your work with a partner.

5. Timely Words The adverb **daily** means "each day." Write what each of these these words means:
a) weekly   b) monthly   c) annually

For each word, name something that happens during that time. For example: **daily** – sun rises.

DID YOU KNOW ?

Etymology (from the Greek word for truth, **etymos**) is the study of word origins and how words developed.

6. Walk Slowly, Happily ... Make a **Word Web** of -ly **adverbs** that describe the word **walk**. See an example of a Word Web on page 62 in Lesson 15.

QUICK TIP

Usually you just add **-ly** to a word. Here are the exceptions:
• Words that end in **y** change **y** to **i** (**daily**).
• You can't have 3 **l**'s in a row (**fully**).
• Most words ending in **le** drop the **e** and add **y** (**gently**).

7. **A Little Alliteration** You use **alliteration** when you include words in sentences or phrases that start with the same sound.

> A **sn**ippy, **sn**appy, **sn**eaky squirrel.

Make an alliteration for 3 of your Lesson Words.

8. **Adjectives and Adverbs** When **-ly** is added to an **adjective** (word that describes a noun) or **noun**, the new word is usually an **adverb**, a word that describes an action. For example:

(adjective)   (noun)
The **brave girl** clung to the edge of the cliff.

(adverb)   (verb)
The girl **bravely clung** to the edge of the cliff.

Write 3 sentences using Lesson Words to describe how an action was done. Don't forget to **proofread**!

9. **As Quickly as ...** Complete these phrases in your notebook, adding the missing **-ly** adverbs.
   a) falls as _____ as a snowflake
   b) talked _____ and _____ on the telephone
   c) smiled _____ and _____
   d) felt _____

   TRY THIS! Turn each phrase into a sentence. For example: Nadia yelled **loudly** and **excitedly** when she won the prize.

AT HOME

10. **Daily Duties** List 15 things you do daily. Rank, from 1 to 5, the top 5 things you like to do each day.

1. wake up reluctantly

2. brush my teeth thoroughly

Focus on Language ▶ Sentence Variety

Use different types of sentences to give your stories variety:
- **statements:**   Today is sunny.
- **questions:**   Where is the sunscreen?
- **exclamations:** Don't get sunburnt!

Combine separate sentences that have related ideas into longer, smoother ones. Combine sentences with **co-ordinating conjunctions** (**and**, **but**, **or**, **for**, **yet**, **so**, **nor**).
- **separate:**   The sun shone. The sky was clear.
- **combined:**   The sun shone **and** the sky was clear.
- **separate:**   The sky was cloudy. It did not rain.
- **combined:**   The sky was cloudy, **but** it did not rain.

Combine sentences with **phrases**.
- **separate:**   We dived into the surf. We screamed.
- **combined:**   **With a scream**, we dived into the surf.
- **separate:**   Tina grabbed her surfboard. She ran into the waves.
- **combined:**   **Grabbing her surfboard**, Tina ran into the waves.

1. Look at the picture on page 86. Write a statement, a question, and an exclamation for the picture. Label each sentence as a **statement**, **question**, or **exclamation**.

2. Combine each group of sentences using (**1**) a **co-ordinating conjunction** and (**2**) a **phrase**:
 a) The dog rolled over. He played dead.
 b) I found the missing key. I used a flashlight.
 c) The lion roared. It charged the car. They drove away.

3. Choose a paragraph you have written recently. Use sentence variety to make it more interesting and easier to read.

FLASHBACK

How can you remember to use adverbs in your story writing?

24 SPELL CHECK

Creating Your Word List

In your notebook

- Go to your list of "Words I Still Need to Practise."
- Pick 12 words you need to practise spelling. These are
  your Review Lesson Words.

Zoom in on Your Words

1. **Say It!** Say each Review Lesson Word slowly.
   Listen for the letter pattern in each **syllable**.

2. **Circle It!** Draw a circle around the part of the
   word you need to focus on.

3. **Missing Letters** Make a missing letter puzzle
   for 5 of your Review Lesson Words. Use your
   spelling strategies to check each spelling.

4. **Digging Up Roots** Underline any **root words** in
   your words. Use these to help you remember the
   spelling.

5. **Bumblebee** Play the Bumblebee game with a partner. Player
   A chooses a Lesson Word and writes down a dash for each
   letter of the word. Player B has to figure out the word by
   suggesting 1 word at a time. Only 1 guess of the final word is
   allowed. For every incorrect guess, Player A draws another part
   of the bumblebee. Then switch roles. Watch out for the stinger!

6. **Practise!** Look at the Strategy Spot on page 31 of Lesson 7.
   Use some of the ideas to study your Review Lesson Words.

7. Compare and Contrast Copy and write the missing **-er** adjectives to complete these sentences in your notebook.

    a) The truck is loud, but the jet is _____ .

    b) This question is difficult, but that one is _____ .

    c) Today is beautiful, but yesterday was _____ .

    d) This watch is tiny, but that one is _____ .

    e) Your answer was good, but hers was _____ .

8. Double Meanings Write 2 sentences for each of these words. Have each sentence show a different meaning.

    a) ground   **b)** sound   **c)** goal   **d)** tough

AT HOME

9. Kitchen Syllables Look around your kitchen and collect 10 words of 2 or more **syllables**.

10. Proofreading Practice Pick the correct spelling in each row. Then use each word in an interesting sentence. Use the strategy on page 87 in Lesson 22 to **proofread** each sentence.

    a) carfully   carefully   carefuly

    b) usual   usaul   usuall

    c) mounten   mountain   mountian

    d) yunger   yonger   younger

11. Writing Descriptively Lana is making a list of describing words for a poem she is working on. Help Lana find 5 **-ly** words to describe:

    a) an elephant walking   **b)** a lion's roar

    c) a teacher's voice   **d)** a cat's meow

12. A Lovely Alliterative List Write **alliterations** for 3 of your Review Lesson Words.

FLASHBACK

Look at the Review Lesson Words you now know how to spell. Cross them off your list of "Words I Still Need to Practise." Hurrah! You're a real spelling champion.

Sometimes do YOU ever feel lost on the "information highway"?

Too Much Information!

cell phones and e-mail link folks far away
maybe we'll run out of things to say
computers get faster and cheaper and smaller —
data banks filled a room, now they fit on a dollar!
without computer graphics, reports just don't fly —
photographs, video clips, and charts to try!
what next? my doggie pet on the Internet?
what more? an elephant faxing the peanut store?

— Samantha Morse

Notice the words with the **"f" sound**. What ways were this sound spelled?

Creating Your Word List

WORD BOX

phoned
photocopy
phrase
telephone
telegraph
sphere
graphics
phase
amphibian
photography
autograph
photograph

Say these words:

phoned phrase telegraph

What sound do these words have in common? What 2 letters produce the **sound** of **"f"**?

1. Make a class list of words that have the **ph sound**. As you read each word in the list out loud, STRESS the **ph sound**.

2. Work with your teacher to create the list of **ph** words you will be learning to spell.
You can use: the Word Box, the poem, your own words.

3. **In your notebook**
   • Write the Lesson Words and underline the **ph sound**.
   • Keep adding **ph** words and challenge words to your Personal Dictionary List. Keep it up to date.

Study Your Spelling Words

English can be a challenging language to spell. Some words do not follow any spelling rules. For example, the words because, should, and weird are challenge words.

1. Make a list of 4 words that are **challenge words.**

2. Look at your list of **challenge words.** Underline the parts of each word that you find EASY to spell. Say each word to yourself.

3. Add other **challenge words** to the list.

4. Keep the list close by when you are writing stories so that you can check the spelling of any **challenge words.**

5. Show your list to someone at home and see what words cause her or him problems. Can you help that person spell 1 of these **challenge words?**

Zoom in on Your Words

1. **Graphic Sort** Sort your Lesson Words on a chart like this. Some of your words will fit into more than 1 column.

photo-	tele-	-graph	other **ph** words

TRY THIS! For an extra challenge, add at least 2 more words to each column on the chart.

2. **Finish It** Use the Word Box to complete these sentences in your notebook.
   a) We shaped clay into a _____ to show the sun in our model of the solar system.
   b) My computer has a _____ program for doing designs.
   c) "Ready or not" is her favourite _____ .
   d) Alexander Graham Bell invented the _____ .
   e) Tara asked her favourite figure skater to _____ the _____ she took of her.

97

When you create words with the **prefix tele-**, you do not usually change the spelling of the word you add it to:
**tele + phone = telephone,
tele + graph = telegraph,
tele + vision = television**.

3. **Tele-photo-graph** The **prefix tele-** means "over a distance." **Photo-** means "light," and the **suffix -graph** means "something written or drawn." Create a "Word Explosion" of related words that contain **tele-**, **photo-**, and **-graph**. Check your words in a dictionary.

4. **Scrambled Syllables** The telephone message got scrambled. Unscramble the syllables to make **ph** words.
   a) phone e tel
   b) to graph pho
   c) cop pho y to
   d) bet al pha
   e) graph to au
   f) an i am phib

   TRY THIS! For an extra challenge, choose 4 of your words and draw small pictures to illustrate each one.

5. **f or ph?** Help Phyllis fill in the missing **f** or **ph** to complete these words. The clues will help you. Write the words in your notebook. When you are done, add **ph** to the **blue** letters to make another name for a ghost.
   a) an old-fashioned record player   __ onograph
   b) a fake   __ ony
   c) $9 \times 5 =$ __ orty-five
   d) a part of a whole   __ raction
   e) a drugstore   __ armacy

DID YOU KNOW?

Even famous authors have trouble with spelling. Today, authors have editors, but years ago they had to proofread their own work. You can still find novels from the 1930s with spelling mistakes writers missed!

AT HOME

6. **Keep in Touch** Interview 2 people at home. Find out how they would communicate with someone a long distance away if they did not have a telephone. How many ways could they keep in touch?

7. **ph Detective** Pick a Lesson Word and write clues to describe it. For example: This is a "far off" written word. Answer: What is a **telegraph**? Read your clues to a partner and see if he or she can guess your Lesson Word.
   TRY THIS! For an extra challenge, do this with 3 more Lesson Words.

Focus on Language ▶ Comparisons

You can write comparisons of 2 unlike things. A **simile** compares one thing to another by using the words **like** or **as**:

The burned-out forest looked like an ugly scar.
I'm as busy as a bee.

1. Choose the words below that will complete these comparisons. Write the completed comparisons in your notebook. Be careful, some of the words are not used!
   a) as _____ as a bug
   b) as _____ as a goose
   c) hungry like a _____
   d) as _____ as a peacock
   e) as _____ as a swan
   f) _____ like the wind

proud snug graceful run silly wolf sly fall bird

2. Complete these similes using your own ideas. Be as imaginative as you can!
   a) as hungry as …
   b) as stubborn as …
   c) as loud as …
   d) walked like …
   e) ran like …
   f) fell like …

3. Use a simile to complete each sentence:
   a) The wind was …
   b) The moon was …
   c) The clouds were …
   d) The noisy children were …

4. Choose a paragraph you have written or read recently. Rewrite it, using similes to make it more interesting to read.

FLASHBACK

Remember: the **ph** pattern usually says "**f**." Which **ph** word(s) did you add to your Personal Dictionary List?

When was the last time you were confused? Think of words that mean the same as **confused**. For example: **perplexed**, **baffled**, **puzzled**, and **bewildered**. Brainstorm 3 more words that are synonyms of **confused**.

Creating Your Word List

WORD BOX

arrived
followed
guessed
seemed
coloured
rounded
slipped
grabbed
fried
tried

Say these words:

rounded   slipped   tried

What sound does **-ed** make in each word? The word part **-ed** is a **suffix**. When you add the **suffix -ed** to the end of a **verb**, you make the **past tense** (happen**ed** in the past).

1. List words that have the **suffix -ed**. Read the words out loud and pay attention to the sound of **-ed** in each word.

2. Work with your teacher to create the list of **-ed** Lesson Words you will be learning to spell.
You can use: the Word Box, the photo, your own words.
Add these 2 words to your Lesson Words:

started, listened

These 2 words are **challenge words**.

3. In your notebook
- Write the Lesson Words and underline the **suffix -ed**.
- Keep adding **-ed** words to your Personal Dictionary List.

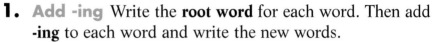

E-x-a-g-g-e-r-a-t-e!

Slowly, and in an exaggerated way, say "I grabbed 10 coloured markers!" Emphasize the syllables so you can actually hear every sound.

Zoom in on Your Words

1. Add -ing Write the **root word** for each word. Then add **-ing** to each word and write the new words.

   a) rounded   **b)** coloured   **c)** listened

   d) started   **e)** followed   **f)** guessed

2. Read All About It! Create 3 newspaper headlines using Lesson Words.

   TRY THIS! For an extra challenge, use 2 or more Lesson Words in the SAME headline. For example: **Skater tried tricky jump but slipped**

3. What's My Rule? Read over each group of words. Match each group to the rule it follows when **-ed** is added.

     • Change the **y** to **i**.
     • Double the final consonant.
     • Just add **-ed**.

  1 slip/slipped, grab/grabbed, step/stepped

  2 seem/seemed, follow/followed, colour/coloured

  3 try/tried, fry/fried, copy/copied

4. Exploding Words! Watch the word **dry** "explode"!

dried   dries   dry   undried   drying

Explode the words below by adding **-s**, **-ed**, **-ing**, **un-**, and so on. Write as many new words as you can. You may need to use a dictionary to make sure each new word makes sense.

a) try   **b)** start   **c)** listen   **d)** open

QUICK TIP

Words ending in **x** are e**x**ceptions; they stay the same when endings are added: fix**ed**, fix**er**, fix**ing**. Words that end in **double consonants** (like **add**) stay the same. (English never has 3 of the same letters in a row.)

5. y to i Add **-ed** to the following words. Use each new word in an interesting sentence. Remember to **proofread**.
   a) cry   **b)** copy   **c)** bury   **d)** apply

6. Bumblebee Play Bumblebee with a partner. Player A chooses a Lesson Word and writes down a dash for each letter of the word. Player B has to figure out the word by suggesting 1 word at a time. Only 1 guess of the final word is allowed. For every incorrect guess, Player A draws another part of the bumblebee. Then switch roles. Watch out for that stinger!

7. Syllable Count Quietly snap, clap, or tap out the syllables in each of your Lesson Words. Copy each word into your notebook, breaking it into **syllables**.

8. Change-a-Consonant Change these words by replacing the **bold consonant** with a different consonant.
   a) tea**m**   **b)** **h**air   **c)** thin**g**
   d) to**y**   **e)** car**t**   **f)** **t**ime
   TRY THIS! Write 3 of your own Change-a-Consonant words and have a partner try to make the new words.

9. More Than One Copy and make the following words **plural**. Use your Does It Look Right? strategy to help you decide whether to add **-s** or **-es**.
   a) colour   **b)** follow   **c)** guess   **d)** agree
   e) fry   **f)** listen   **g)** tax   **h)** try

AT HOME

10. Colour Your World People use many words to describe colour. For example, there is **grass green**, **mossy green**, and **lime green**. Choose your favourite colour and brainstorm a list of words and phrases that could describe different shades of that colour.

Focus on Language ▶ Vigorous Verbs

Authors vary the words they use to give more exact meanings and to keep readers interested. For example, the verb **went** can be expressed many different ways:

> depart   leave   exit   disappear

1. Write a sentence for each **went** word.

2. This story needs help! Make it more exciting to read by finding alternate words for **to go**. Use the new verbs and rewrite the story beginning.

> Jeff **went** to check up on his snake. He noticed that the lid was off the terrarium. He **went** around the room. Then he saw it! Before he got to it, the snake **went** ...

Share your story beginning with a partner and **proofread** it together.

3. Signs often use vigorous verbs to emphasize a point. In this sign, verbs are used to emphasize the idea of **moving carefully**.

> Please DO NOT run, rush, jump, skip, jog, scamper, dash, spring, or scurry in the store.

Complete this sign in your notebook by adding more verbs. Use a **thesaurus** if you need help.

> (in a library) Please DO read, enjoy , _____ , _____ , _____ , and _____ our books.

Make up your own sign, using verbs to emphasize an idea.

4. The words **mad** and **went** are overused. Look over your own writing and list other words that need to be replaced.

FLASHBACK

You have learned several things about words that end in the **suffix -ed**. Write down 3 things you learned in this lesson.

See how the jigsaw puzzle pieces make new words.

The **suffix -ment** means "the result of" or "the condition of."
Adding **-ment** to a **verb** turns it into a **noun**: **disagree** ("to quarrel") + **-ment** = **disagreement** (the result of a quarrel).

Creating Your Word List

Say these words:
Say the new word created when the **suffix -ment** is added to:

1. List words that have the **suffix -ment**. Use the jigsaw puzzle to help you.

2. Work with your teacher to create the list of **-ment** words you will be learning to spell.
    You can use: the Word Box, the puzzle, your own words.
    As you read each word in the list out loud, STRESS **-ment**.

3. **In your notebook**
    • Write the Lesson Words and underline the **suffix -ment**.
    • Add **-ment** words to your Personal Dictionary List.

WORD BOX

apartment
basement
equipment
document
excitement
disagreement
settlement
agreement
payment
judgement
enjoyment
experiment

Zoom in on Your Words

1. **Meant to Enjoy** Write the **root word** for each word. Then add **-ment** to each word and write the new words.

    a) paying   **b)** based   **c)** exciting

    d) settler   **e)** enjoying   **f)** judges

2. **Word Sort** Copy this chart and use your Lesson Words and other **-ment** words you know to complete it.

root word	+ ment	+ other endings
pay	payment	pays, paying

3. **Missing Letters** Copy and add the missing letters and complete these Word Box words in your notebook.

    a) p _ _ m _ nt   **b)** _ nj _ yme _ _   **c)** _ xc _ t _ m _ nt

    d) d _ _ u _ _nt   **e)** ba _ e _ _ _ t   **f)** s _ tt _ _ me _ _

4. **Match Up!** Match each word with its meaning:

    1 payment   **a)** a room or rooms for living in

    2 experiment   **b)** a paper giving important information

    3 document   **c)** an amount paid

    4 settlement   **d)** a test to find out what will happen

    5 apartment   **e)** a small community of homes

    TRY THIS! For an extra challenge, make clues for 3 other Lesson Words. Share them with a partner.

STRATEGY SPOT

STRESS Syllables!

When we say a word with more than 1 syllable, we say 1 part of the word slightly louder than the others. We **stress** that syllable. Say these words. Notice the sound of each **stressed syllable**: en • **JOY** • ment, **SET** • tle • ment, **PAY** • ment.

5. **Syllable STRESS** Break each word into **syllables**. Write the stressed syllable in CAPITAL LETTERS.

    a) excited   **b)** excitement   **c)** basement

    d) judgement   **e)** document   **f)** disagreement

6. Finish the Statements Use the Word Box to complete these sentences in your notebook.
   a) The judge made a _____ after hearing the case.
   b) The crowd was cheering with _____ after the goal.
   c) Lisa went down to the _____ to get the hose.
   d) The coach brought out the gymnastics _____ .
   e) There was a _____ between the batter and the umpire about the pitch.

7. Exploding Words! Watch the word **suit** "explode"!

Explode these words. Check your new words.
a) excite   **b)** agree   **c)** pay   **d)** equip

8. It's a Challenge! Choose the correct **homophone** from the pairs to complete the sentences.
   a) Did you know that (**their/there**) team (**won/one**)?
   b) What is the name of (**their/they're**) team's mascot?
   c) I (**new/knew**), but I'm not (**quiet/quite**) sure now.
   d) (**It's/Its**) a bear, but I don't know (**it's/its**) name.
   e) I bet (**you're/your**) (**write/right**).

AT HOME

9. Summer Vacation What will you do during your summer vacation? Brainstorm **-ment** words that describe your feelings about your summer vacation.

10. Foldover Fold a piece of paper like a fan. Make 6 folds. Print a Lesson Word on the first fold. Fold over so you can't see the word. On the next fold write the word again. Open up the paper and check your spelling. Repeat practising your word on each fold. Be sure to check for the correct spelling each time you write the word. See p. 10 for an example of a foldover.

DID YOU KNOW ?

The word **document** has no root word in English. The **suffix -ment** was added to the Latin word **docere**, "to teach."

Focus on Language ▶ Dictionary Skills

When you look up words in the dictionary, it helps to think, "Is the word near the beginning, or near the end of the book?" You can imagine your dictionary divided into 2 parts: **a** to **m**, and **n** to **z**. We call **a–m section 1** of the alphabet, and **n–z section 2**.

1. Write the Lesson Words that you would find in **section 1** (**a–m**).

2. Write the Lesson Words that you would find in **section 2** (**n–z**).

3. Complete these sentences in 2 ways. First, with a word from **section 1** of the dictionary (**a–m**). Second, with a word from **section 2** (**n–z**).
   a) Her favourite sport is ...
   b) His favourite food is ...
   c) Something great about me is that I'm ...

One way to find words quickly in the dictionary is to use the 2 **guide words** at the top of each page. The first guide word tells you the first word on the dictionary page. The other guide word is the last entry word. For example:

hamster ▶	**happy**

4. Use your dictionary and write the 2 guide words at the top of the page where each of these words is found:
   a) apartment   **b)** basement   **c)** judgement
   d) leopard   **e)** excitement   **f)** whose

5. Find 5 interesting words in the dictionary. See if your partner can find them using **sections** and **guide words**.

FLASHBACK

Think about the last time you used a dictionary. What made it difficult to find a word? What made it easy?

Read this poem and visualize the picture the author is creating.

The Duck

Behold the duck.
It does not cluck.
A cluck it lacks.
It quacks.
It is specially fond.
Of a puddle or a pond.
When it dines or sups.
It bottoms ups.

— Ogden Nash

Creating Your Word List

WORD BOX

cricket
stock
stuck
thick
flicker
track
picnic
clinic
basic
plastic
mechanic
fantastic

Say these words:

stick   track   picnic   basic

How would you describe the **"k" sound**? Is it a "hard" sound?

1. Make a list of words that have the **"k" sound**. Use the poem to help you. Put the words into a chart like this:

-ic	ck

2. Work with your teacher to create the list of **-ic** and **ck** Lesson Words you will be learning to spell.
You can use: the Word Box, the poem, your own words.

3. In your notebook
   • Write the Lesson Words and highlight the **"k" sound**.
   • Add **-ic** and **ck** words to your Personal Dictionary List.

Zoom in on Your Words

1. Framed! Use a coloured pencil to draw the **wordprint** shape of each Lesson Word.

2. Word Clinic Fix these "**k**" **sound** words by completing them in your notebook.

  a) cri _ _ et **b)** fl _ _ ker **c)** _ _ ast _ _

  d) stu _ _ **e)** tr _ _ k **f)** me _ _ an _ _

STRATEGY

SPOT **Using a Computer Spellcheck**

A computer spellcheck can be a quick way to correct spelling mistakes. To use a spellcheck successfully, you must:
  a) spell enough of the word correctly for it to recognize the word
  b) know the meaning of the word you want to spell
  c) be able to recognize the correct spelling in a list

3. Spellcheck For each misspelled Word Box word, the spellcheck listed 2 possible words. Pick the correct spelling.

misspelled word	spellcheck suggestions
a) fliker	flier flicker
b) pincnic	pink picnic
c) fantastik	fantasy fantastic

QUICK TIP

You need to add a **k** to words that end in **-ic** before endings like **-ed** and **-ing**: **panic**, **panicked**, **panicking**.

4. Change-a-Letter Change 1 letter in each of these words to make a new word.

  a) thick **b)** stock **c)** track

  d) lock **e)** sick **f)** click

  TRY THIS! For an extra challenge, change 2 or more letters in the following words to make new words.

  g) block **h)** flicker **i)** cricket

5. Word Pole Copy and complete this Word Pole. Use the clues to write Word Box words. The word in the pole will tell what you should NOT do in an emergency.

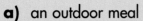

a) an outdoor meal
b) simple, but important
c) a medical centre
d) shine unsteadily
e) an insect; also a game

a) _ |_ _ _ _ _
b) _ |_ _ _ _
c) _ _ _ |_ _ _
d) _ _ |_ _ _ _ _
e) _ |_ _ _ _ _ _

6. Double Exposure The word **cricket** has 2 meanings — an insect and a game. What 2 meanings does the word **track** have? Write sentences to show the different meanings of **cricket** and **track**.

> **DID YOU KNOW?**
>
> A **modem** lets computers communicate by telephone. It **modulates** (changes computer signals into sound signals) to connect to a phone line. It also picks up sound signals and **demodulates** them (changes them back into computer signals).

AT HOME

7. Word Web Pick 1 of your Lesson Words. What 2 other words come to mind? Add as many words as you can to make a Word Web.

8. Elemenno/LMNO! Pick a Lesson Word. Start with the FIRST letter of your word, then write the next 4 letters of the alphabet. Use words that start with those 5 letters to make a silly sentence. Write 2 more Elemennos. Like this:

My **n**ew **o**range **p**yjamas **q**uack!

FLASHBACK

What have you noticed about the position of the **-ic** and **ck patterns** in words?

TECHNOLOGY

E-Mail Me!

Communicating through computer e-mail (electronic mail) lets you send a letter at the speed of light. A modem connects your computer to telephone lines. Since it is usually written quickly, e-mail is not as formal as a regular letter. Here is a sample e-mail message:

From: samaya@interlog.com
Subject: Spelling book
To: jrowsell@nelson.com
Dear Jennifer, Just saw grade 6 spelling book.
Looks great! Let me know when 7 is printed.
BFN, Alan. :-)

In the "To" and "From" addresses, the code names "samaya" and "jrowsell" identify the people communicating. There are lots of Alans and Jennifers, so these users have chosen special **usernames**. The symbol @ means "at." The last word, **com**, shows that the computer is part of a **commercial** organization. This is its **domain** name. Here are some other domains:

> edu = educational (school, college, university)
> gov = government
> ca = Canada
> BFN is short for "Bye for now," and the symbol :-) means
> the sender is happy, or joking. This is called a **smiley**.

1. Write your own e-mail message. Be sure to include a **username** and a **domain** name in the addresses.

2. Make up 3 of your own shortcut messages similar to **BFN**.

3. Does your school use e-mail? If so, what is its e-mail address?

4. If you have a computer at school or at home that can send e-mail, practise sending messages to someone else who has e-mail.

Look what can happen if you don't pay attention to the beginning sounds of words.

Stringbean Small

Stringbean Small was tall and trim,
basketball seemed meant for him.
at eight foot four, a coach's dream,
And yet he failed to make the team.

It seems at practice, Stringbean Small
began to chew the basketball,
the coach screamed, "Stop! Don't nibble it!
I wanted you to *dribble* it!"

— Jack Prelusky

Creating Your Word List

Say these words:
- Say the new word created when the **prefix un-** is added to:
able, fold, natural

The **prefix un-** can mean "not" (**un**able — not able) or "opposite of" (**un**fold — do the opposite of folding).
- Say the new word created when the **prefix re-** is added to:
open, pay, view

The **prefix re-** can mean "again" (**re**open — open again) or "back" (**re**pay — pay back). What does **review** mean?

1. Work with your teacher to create the list of **un-** and **re-** words you will be learning to spell.
You can use: the Word Box, your own words.
These are your Lesson Words.

2. In your notebook
- Write the Lesson Words and highlight the **prefixes**.
- Add **un-** and **re-** words to your Personal Dictionary List.

Zoom in on Your Words

1. **Snap, Clap, Tap!** Slowly say each Lesson Word and quietly snap, clap, or tap out the **syllables**.

2. **Unidentified Words!** Using each letter only once, see how many words you can make from the letters in **unidentified**.

3. **Not, Opposite!** Add the **prefix un-** to the words. Then write either **not** or **do opposite** beside each new word. Like this:

   unhappy – **not**   unfold – **do opposite**

   a) able   **b)** packed   **c)** natural
   d) tie   **e)** certain   **f)** do

4. **Back Again?** Copy these Lesson Words. Then write either **again** or **back** beside each word. Like this:

   reopen – **again**   repay – **back**

   a) rewrite   **b)** reward   **c)** review
   d) recall   **e)** reply   **f)** redo

   TRY THIS! For an extra challenge, break each word into syllables in your notebook. Use a coloured pencil to add the hyphens (-) between syllables.

QUICK TIP

Always add the prefix to the WHOLE word. That will prevent you from missing letters in words like **mis**spell, **un**natural, and **re**entry.

DID YOU KNOW?

Words like **remember, reply,** and **respond** do not seem to have **root words**. That's because the **prefix** was already part of the Latin words they came from. Many dictionaries will give you the origins of these seemingly "rootless" words.

STRATEGY SPOT

Start with the Root Word

If you are not sure how to spell a word, begin by spelling just the root word. To find a word in the dictionary, you can look up its root word.

5. Rerun Have a word race with a partner. Set up 2 columns on your paper with **re-** and **un-** headings. In 3 minutes, write as many words as you can, beginning with these prefixes. Share and compare with a partner.

6. Word Formulas Complete these formulas to write the new words.

a) un + tie – e + ed =   **b)** reminding – re – ing + ful =
c) un + love – e + able =   **d)** re + write – e + t + en =
e) respond – d + se =   **f)** un + identify – y + i + ed =

TRY THIS! For an extra challenge, "explode" each word you made by adding and subtracting endings and prefixes. Check your new words in a dictionary.

7. Proofreading Practice Read the sentences quietly to yourself. Then rewrite each one, correcting the words that do not look right or are the wrong **homophone**.

   a) They unpacked there suitcases to get ready for the trip.
   b) Their is no food in the refrigerate.
   c) I rewrite my poem to times too make it rhyme.
   d) Have your ever see an identifying fliing object?

8. Concentration Cut a sheet of paper into 20 equal-sized squares. Write your Lesson Words twice — 1 word per square. Turn the squares over and mix them up. Number the **back** of the squares from 1 to 20. Take turns turning over 2 numbers until you get a pair of matching words.

AT HOME

9. A Wordy Collage Look through old magazines and newspapers to find words that start with **un-** and **re-**, and other interesting words. Cut out the words and arrange them different ways on a piece of paper. Once you have an arrangement you like, glue the words onto the paper. Give your collage a title. Add pictures if you want. Have fun!

FLASHBACK

What are some of the ways our study of **root words** and **prefixes** has helped you become a better speller?

Sports Talk

> He hits the blueline in full flight, winds up the top of the circle, and drills one ...

> It's the last minute of play, the defenceman slides across, deflects the puck into the boards ...

Can you tell what kind of sports event these 2 announcers are covering? Sports use words in special ways. Each sport has special names for the players' positions, the playing area, the divisions of play, and so on. And each team has its own nickname (Canucks, Raptors).

SPORTS TERMS

	hockey	baseball	soccer	basketball
when you score it's called a ...	goal			basket
the game is divided into ...	periods			
the playing area is called a ...				
the player positions are ...				
our favourite team's nickname is ...				

1. As a group, copy and complete the chart. What other terms can you add to the chart? You can add pictures and make the chart part of a Sports Talk Poster!

2. Find 2 articles from the sports section of the newspaper or a magazine. Highlight special sports terms and phrases. Use your spelling strategies to practise challenging words.

115

SPELL CHECK

Patterns
ph
suffix -ed
suffix -ment
-ic, ck
prefixes un-, re-

Strategies

1. List challenge words.
2. Exaggerate!
3. Stress syllables!
4. Using a computer spellcheck.
5. Start with the root word.

Creating Your Word List

In your notebook
- Go to your list of "Words I Still Need to Practise."
- Pick 12 words you need to practise spelling. These are your Review Lesson Words.

Zoom in on Your Words

1. **Say It!** Say each Review Lesson Word in an e-x-a-g-g-e-r-a-t-e-d way. Listen for the sound of each letter pattern.

2. **Show It!** Use a coloured pencil to highlight the part of each word you need to focus on.

3. **Digging Up Roots** Underline any **root words** in your words. Use these to help you remember the spelling.

4. **Proofreading Practice** Pick the correct spelling in each row. Then use 4 of the words in interesting sentences. Use the strategy on page 87 in Lesson 22 to **proofread** your sentences.

a) telefone	telphone	telephone
b) guessed	guesed	geussed
c) follwoed	followed	folowed
d) garphics	grafics	graphics
e) basement	bassement	basment
f) ecxiting	exciting	exiting

5. **You Don't Say!** Michael is editing his ghost story and he just realized he used the word **said** too many times. Give Michael a list of 10 other words he can use for **said**.

6. All Sorts Write each of your Review Words on a small piece of paper. Think of different ways to sort your words: Sort by letter pattern, sort by sound, sort by meaning.

7. E-mail It Write a message about your favourite activity in this lesson that you could e-mail to a friend.
TRY THIS! If you have access to a computer with e-mail, practise sending messages back and forth with someone you know who has e-mail too. Be careful to type **usernames** correctly — no capitals and no spaces:

me@myschool.ca

AT HOME

8. Practise! Look at the Strategy Spot on page 31 of Lesson 7. Use some of the ideas to study your Review Lesson Words.

9. Word Stairs Write down a Lesson Word or other word you can spell. Your partner uses the last letter of the word to start the next word. Take turns to see how far you can make the stairs go. Do it like this:

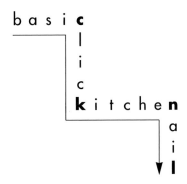

FLASHBACK

Look at the Review Lesson Words you now know how to spell. Cross them off your list of "Words I Still Need to Practise." You are in good spelling shape! Keep those spelling muscles strong! Make a "Keep fit" spelling plan for yourself.

It's time to review what we have learned about silent letters.
Can you find all the silent letters in these goofy knock-knock jokes?

Knock, knock.
— Who's there?
Orange.
— Orange who?
Orange you glad
I'm here.

Knock, knock.
— Who's there?
Doughnut.
— Doughnut who?
Doughnut climb the tree.

Knock, knock.
— Who's there?
Gus.
— Gus who?
Gus who's coming
to dinner.

WORD BOX

straight
weigh
stalk
know
whistle
knock
limb
height
two
wrong
doubt
sign
scissors
writer
slice

Creating Your Word List

Say these words:

weigh · know · limb · stalk

All of these words have **silent letters**. Which letters are seen but
not heard?

1. As a class, make a list of words that have **silent letters**.
Use the knock-knock jokes to help you. Put the words into
a chart like this:

silent letter at beginning	silent letter at end	silent letter in the middle

2. Work with your teacher to create a list of **silent letter** words you will be learning to spell.
You can use: the Word Box, the jokes, your own words. These are your Lesson Words.

3. In your notebook
- Write the Lesson Words. Underline the **silent letters**.
- Can you find some words in your Personal Dictionary List that have **silent letters**?

QUICK TIP

Two is commonly misspelled. To help remember the silent **w**, think of **two** with its related words **twice, twins, twelve, twenty**.

Zoom in on Your Words

1. Word Sort Sort the words from the Word Box into this chart.

silent k	silent g	silent b	silent h	silent l

2. Crack the Code Copy each sentence and complete each word that is missing silent letters.
- **a)** I will w_is_le to let you _now where I am.
- **b)** To get to the museum, go strai_ _t and turn at the wrou_ _t-iron fence.
- **c)** I dou _t you are _rong.
- **d)** Lis_en carefully! You mi_ _t be a ha_f asleep.
- **e)** Be sure to wei_ _ yourself before your vacation.

AT HOME

3. **Silent Letter Search** Look for 20 words at home with silent letters and underline the silent letters.

4. **Hidden Words** Draw a picture like the one below to illustrate more **silent letter** words.

5. **Stock and Stalk** **Homophones** are words that sound the same but are spelled differently and have different meanings. For example:

<blockquote>
Jack climbed up the bean stalk.
Don't forget to add chicken stock to your stew.
</blockquote>

Use each of the following **homophone pairs** in a sentence. Like this:

<blockquote>
where/wear —
My friend said, "Where will you ever wear that!"
</blockquote>

a) know/no   **b)** way/weigh   **c)** two/too

6. **Wake the sleeping b!** In words that end in **-mb** and **-bt** the **b** is silent. Wake the sleeping **b** and copy and solve these riddles. The clues will help you.

a) part of a tree	**a)** _ _ _ _
b) one of your fingers	**b)** _ _ _ _ _
c) how to get up a tree	**c)** _ _ _ _ _
d) a very small piece of bread	**d)** _ _ _ _ _

TRY THIS! For an extra challenge, make clues for 3 of your Lesson Words. Share them with a partner.

7. **Silly Silent Sentences** With a partner, write 5 silly sentences using as many words with **silent letters** as you can. For example: Mark whis**t**les before he wei**gh**s himself.

Focus on Language ▶ Verb Tenses

Verbs are time-tellers. They have different forms, called **tenses**, that help you place an event in time. There are 3 **simple tenses** in English — **past**, **present**, **future**. The **simple future tense** uses the helping verb **will**.

Past Tense Something **happened** in the past		Present Tense Something **happens** right now		Future Tense Something will **happen** in the future.	
	Present	**Present Participle**	**Past**	**Past Participle**	
Regular Verbs These verbs form the simple past tense by adding **-ed** or **-d**. Most verbs are like this, for example:	jump	is jumping	jumped	has jumped	
Irregular Verbs These verbs form the past tense in different ways. Here are some **irregular verbs**:	be bring break eat	is being is bringing is breaking is eating	was, were brought broke ate	has been has brought has broken has eaten	

1. Copy the chart in your notebook. Use your spelling strategies to practise spelling **irregular verbs** in the chart.

2. Use the chart and your dictionary to rewrite these sentences. Use the correct form of each verb.
   a) Last month, my dog **run** away.
   b) Lisa **see** it at her neighbour's house after she **hear** it barking.

FLASHBACK

In this lesson, we looked at **silent letter** patterns. Has your list of **silent letter** words helped you with your writing?

Let's look at some prefixes and suffixes from the dictionary. Notice all the things the dictionary tells us about prefixes and suffixes.

com-   or **col-** or **con-** *prefix* with, together, jointly, altogether. *com-* is used before *b*, *m*, *p*, and occasionally before vowels and *f*.

-less   /ləs/ *suffix* forming adjectives and adverbs.

-ment   /mənt/ *suffix* **1** forming nouns expressing the means or result of the action of a verb (*abridgement*; *embankment*).

re-   /ri: re/ *prefix* **1** attachable to almost any verb or its derivative, meaning: **a** once more; afresh, anew (*readjust*; *renumber*).

-ful   /fəl/ *comb. form* forming: **1** adjectives from nouns, meaning: **a** full of (*beautiful*). **b** having qualities of (*masterful*).

WORD BOX

adventurous
careless
communication
completed
disagreement
disease
hoping
information
removable
lovable
mysterious
revision
unidentified
useless
wonderful

Creating Your Word List

Say these words:

disagreement   lovable   unidentified   useless

What sounds do **-less**, **re-**, **-tion**, **un-**, and **-ful** make in each word?

The word part **-less** is a **suffix** and the word part **un-** is a **prefix**. A **suffix** is a group of letters placed at the end of a word. A **prefix** is a group of letters placed at the beginning of a word.

1. List words that have **prefixes** and **suffixes**. Use the dictionary to help you. Read the words out loud and pay attention to the sound of each prefix and suffix.

2. With your teacher create the list of **prefixes** and **suffixes** you will be learning to spell.
    You can use: the Word Box, the dictionary, your own words.

3. In your notebook
- Write the Lesson Words and <u>underline</u> the **prefixes** and **suffixes**.
- Keep adding prefixes and suffixes to your Personal Dictionary List. Have you been keeping it up to date?

STRATEGY SPOT   Add a Prefix to the Whole Word!

Always add a prefix to the whole word. This will prevent you from leaving out letters in words like: immature, reentry, unnatural, missspell.

Zoom in on Your Words

1. **Finish It!** Use the correct form of the word printed in brackets to copy and complete each sentence.
  - **a)** I think you look _____ in red and green. (**wonder**)
  - **b)** They had a _____ about what to do for the project. (**agree**)
  - **c)** Fred saw an _____ flying object last night. (**identify**)
  - **d)** Alan has finally _____ the _____ of his book. (**complete**), (**revise**)
  - **e)** The _____ gentleman ran from sight. (**mystery**)
  - **f)** I am _____ Tara will come to my party. (**hope**)

  TRY THIS! For an extra challenge, write your own sentences using words with **prefixes** and **suffixes**.

2. **Exploding Words** Watch the word joy "explode"!

joyous   joyful   joy   enjoyment   enjoyed   joyfully

Explode these words by writing as many new words as you can. Check in a dictionary to make sure your new words make sense.

a) care   **b)** agree   **c)** sign   **d)** adventure

QUICK TIP

If you add **till** or **full** to a word, drop one **l**. For example: full – joyful.

3. **Find the Beginning and Ending** In your notebook, match the root words with the **prefixes** and **suffixes** listed below. Then add a different **prefix** or **suffix** to make a new word.

Root Words	Prefixes	Suffixes
ease	in-	-ful
love	re-	-ment
agree	un-	-ous
form	dis-	-able

AT HOME

4. **The Newspaper Hunt** Look in a newspaper to find 10 **prefixes** and **suffixes** and list the words.
TRY THIS! Use your 10 words in interesting sentences.

5. **Heard it through the grapevine ...** Match the root words with the **prefixes** and **suffixes** in the grapes.

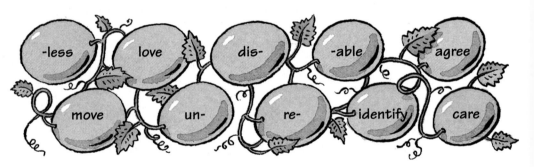

6. **Word Addition** Give yourself one point for each of the following words that you write correctly with a **prefix** or **suffix**. For each word that you write correctly with BOTH a **prefix** and a **suffix**, give yourself 3 points.

a) form	**b)** possible	**c)** wonder
d) complete	**e)** contain	**f)** usual
g) interest	**h)** popular	**i)** danger
j) appear	**k)** care	**l)** exhibit

FLASHBACK

Review the strategies you have learned this year. What strategies have you used the most?

Connecting with

MATH

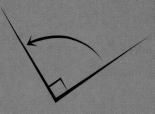

Metric Units

The common base units of our metric system are: metre (length), gram (mass), Litre (volume). We add prefixes to the basic units to create the various units of measurement. Study this illustration:

micro-	milli-	centi-	deci-	0	deca-	hecto-	kilo-	mega-
$\frac{1}{\text{million}}$	$\frac{1}{1000}$	$\frac{1}{100}$	$\frac{1}{10}$		10	100	1000	million

Can you imagine writing out the word **kilogram** or **centimetre** every time you use it? Fortunately, there is a set of easy-to-use **abbreviations** for the metric system. Look at the way each word is abbreviated:

centimetre	cm	millimetre	mm
kilogram	kg	milligram	mg
centiLitre	cL	hectoLitre	hL

First letter of prefix plus first letter of base unit. No period at end.

1. Write out the full name of the unit for each of these measurements:
   a) ten Litres **b)** tenth of a gram **c)** thousand metres
   d) million Litres **e)** hundredth of a gram **f)** millionth of a metre

2. Shorten these metric measurements:
   a) centigram **b)** hectogram **c)** milliLitre
   d) kiloLitre **e)** kilometre **f)** decimetre

3. Choose 3 of the units from Number 2 and draw a picture for each, showing something that might have that measurement.

4. Use your spelling strategies to practise words that are difficult.

Spelling **STRETCH**

Spelling **STRETCH**

Find out more about words and make your spelling skills stretch in this special section of exciting games and extra challenges. Your teacher will show you which activities are just for YOU.

1. **Write It, Right It!**

   a) **Homophones** are words that sound the same as another word but are spelled differently and have different meanings. Read each sentence, and then choose and write the correct homophone:

   1 Do you climb the **stare** or the **stair**?
   2 Does the father have a **sun** or a **son**?
   3 Do you sleep at **night** or **knight**?
   4 Do you ride a **hoarse** or a **horse**?
   5 Is a teddy a **bear** or a **bare**?
   6 When you hurt yourself, are you in **pain** or **pane**?
   7 What do you pick in your garden, a **flour** or a **flower**?
   8 Does the store have a half-price **sale** or **sail**?
   9 When you count, do you start with **one** or **won**?
   10 Is a long, narrow room in the house a **hall** or a **haul**?

   b) Make up 4 of your own homophone questions and give them to a partner to solve.

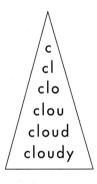

2. **Build Pyramids** Choose a challenge word you want to practise. Use it to make a Word Pyramid. On the first line, print the first letter of the word. On the second line, print the first 2 letters. On the third line, the first 3 letters. Continue until the word is complete.

   a) Build 3 other pyramids, with words that start with (a) the letter **m**, (b) the letter **q**, and (c) the letter **t**.

   b) Make an upside-down pyramid! Start with a whole word, and then subtract 1 letter at a time until you finish with just 1 letter.

3. **Be Positive!** Use mistakes as opportunities for learning. To help you do this, think of some positive things you can say to yourself when you make a spelling mistake. Instead of saying "I always get this wrong," you could say "This mistake shows me I know most of the word."

   a) Draw 3 word balloons and write 3 **positive** things you can say when you've made a spelling mistake.

b) With a partner, think of 3 other situations in which positive thinking would be helpful. For each, write (a) what a person focusing on the **negative** might say, and (b) what could be said to focus on the **positive** instead.

4. Get It Right! Rewrite this story starter, correcting the mistakes in using **verbs** (action words). Remember to use the same **tense** (past, present, or future) throughout!

> Mark is laying at the bottom of the hill. His leg was really sore. He thinks he has breaked it. He's all alone — everyone else are off getting help. Soon it began to get dark. Where is his friends? Lisa and Ali are supposed to come back and saw if he was okay. Luisa should of gotten help by now! Mark checked his watch.

5. Compound Your Fun! The word **compound** means "to increase." Compound words are two words that combine to form a single word. For example:

> *doghouse   turtleneck   catnap*

a) Make up a list of compound words that would be fun to act out.

b) Share your list with a partner and play a game of charades.

6. Descriptive Words When a sound of a word reflects its meaning, this is called **onomatopoeia**. For example:

> Bees **buzz**, dogs **bark**, and cats **meow**.
> The thunder **crashed** and **smashed** across the sky.

a) Find all the words in the duck poem on page 108 in Lesson 28 that have onomatopoeia. Some of the words are made-up words. The reader has to listen to the sound of the words to get the meaning.

b) Brainstorm a list of words that suggest:
1 gently moving water or wind
2 rushing water or strong wind

c) Write a poem using some of the water or wind words. Or you can combine both sets of words.

7. **Prefix Pets** Create a "prefix pet" by combining number prefixes with body-part words.

    a) Use some of the prefixes below and write the names of 5 new creatures.

    b) Draw one of your creatures.

    c) Using the prefix chart, ask a partner to try to guess your creature's name.

Example: A triheaded, decalegged, spiny tailed hexahorn.

Prefixes	**Body-part words**	
1 : uni- or single-	toed	horned
2 : bi- or double-	headed	eyed
3 : tri- or triple-	nosed	eared
4 : quadri-, quadru-, quadr-	tailed	footed
5 : quint- or penta-	legged	clawed
6 : hexa-, hex-		
7 : sept-		
8 : oct-, octa-, octo-		
9 : nona-		
10 : deca-, dec-		
many: poly-		

8. **Shortcuts** Shorten the message by rewriting this story starter using **abbreviations** (shortcut words) for the words printed in **bold**.

On **Monday**, **October fifth**, **at ten-thirty** in the **morning**, **Doctor** Lee checked her **electronic mail**, grabbed her **identification documents**, and hailed a **taxicab**.

"The Airport, **as soon as possible**, please", she said.

She arrived at the **headquarters** of the **Royal Canadian Mounted Police** just in time to pick up the **package** of secret documents. Looking over the papers, she realized that this time she was close. In her files was a **photograph** of an **unidentified flying object**.

9. **Alphabetics!** Pick a letter of the alphabet and make it into a picture of an object that begins with the letter. Write a description and begin each line with the letter you choose.

Snakes

Slither

Silently

10. **Say It a Better Way** RePete is feeling lonely these days. No one wants to talk with him because his conversations are boring — he uses the same dull words over and over. Help make RePete's conversations more interesting. Read the sentences below. Look up the underlined words in a thesaurus. Write a more interesting **synonym** for each word. Then rewrite the sentences.

    a) It's a nice day.
    b) I like hot weather!
    c) It will be fun to go to the game.
    d) This is the big game of the season.
    e) We have the best team!
    f) The other team is bad.
    g) I just love soccer!
    h) I get so happy that I act silly!

11. **I'd Love to Meet ...** Rewrite this sentence, filling in the blanks with 2 rhyming words:

I'd love to meet a _____ that could _____ !

Example: I'd love to meet a **book** that could **cook**!

    a) Write 5 more "I'd love to meet" rhymes.
    b) Pick your best rhyme and draw a picture to illustrate it.

12. **Shhh! Silent Letter Zone** For as many letters in the alphabet as possible, try to find a word with a silent letter. For example:

a is silent in _____ and **b** is silent in **climb**

List the words in your notebook.

13. Housewords

a) Imagine that you are a house and need a dictionary. What words would be important to a house? They might include **window**, **builder**, **foundation**, **room**, **roof**, **basement**, **painter**, and **landscaping**. Write 5 more words that might go in a house dictionary.

b) Write all of the 13 house words in alphabetical order. Beside each word, write its meaning. Add small illustrations to the words that help describe the word.

c) Make a dictionary for 1 of the following household items or choose an item of your own. Make a list of at least 10 words that would be in the item's dictionary. Put the words in alphabetical order, and beside each word write its meaning. Add pictures where you think they would help.

refrigerator	electric drill	kitchen sink
television set	CD player	door

14. Personal PL8's
Sometimes licence plates are personalized with a message or saying. Design 4 personalized licence plates. Each plate can have no more than 8 numbers and/or letters. Use abbreviations, phonetic spelling, letters like C, R, B, U, and numbers like 2 and 4.

15. Leaping Lizards
To describe how lizards move, you could write the colourful phrase "leaping lizards."

a) Choose interesting adjectives to write phrases that describe how each of these animals moves:

1 worm	2 dolphin	3 snake
4 kangaroo	5 elephant	6 grasshopper
7 lion	8 hamster	9 butterfly

b) Use 3 of these phrases in a poem about animal action.

16. Complete the Action
Look back at the story starters in Numbers 4 and 7. Choose one, copy it in your notebook, and use your own ideas to finish the story. Be sure to:
- use sentence variety to add interest and clarity
- use active and precise verbs

- watch your verb tenses and irregular verbs
- use descriptive adjectives, adverbs, and phrases
- avoid repeated words and tired phrases
- give your story a bold, eye-catching title
- proofread your final copy

17. **School-Day Crossword** Find the words that describe some of the things you do, see, and use at school. Write them in your notebook. When you are done, unscramble the letters in the circles to answer this question: **Where do students go at recess?**

Across

1 the study of pictures
3 you read stories in these
5 subject that deals with numbers
7 synonym of **pals**
9 a break between classes
11 subject in which you study nature
12 used to measure things
15 what you are doing in school
17 you write or read these
18 comparison using **like** or **as**
19 where you play indoor sports

Down

2 synonym of **instructors**
4 the month school begins
6 an official language of Canada
8 what this book is about
10 rings at the end of the day
13 the head of a school
14 a complete thought (has a **verb**)
15 this book has 32 of these units
16 to look at carefully

18. **Hot Sun** The goal of this word game is to turn one word into another word, 1 letter at a time. The challenge is to make as many words as possible. For example, you can turn **sun** into **hot** in 4 steps:

sun ↓ **b**un ↓ but ↓ **h**ut ↓ hot

a) Change 1 letter at a time to make 3 more words for each of these words: **east, warm, bin**.

b) Make 4 more words for each of these words: **sick, car, top**.

c) See how many words you can make with the word **hope**. Make AT LEAST 6 more words.

19. **Eat Around the World**

a) Copy the words and match the "adopted" food word with its original language. If a food is new to you, ask your classmates to find out if any of them are familiar with it.

1	lasagna	**a)**	Japanese
2	bagel	**b)**	German
3	croissant	**c)**	Arabic
4	perogy	**d)**	Armenian/Turkish
5	falafel	**e)**	Hungarian
6	squash	**f)**	Spanish
7	schnitzel	**g)**	Ukrainian
8	taco	**h)**	Greek
9	sushi	**i)**	Chinese
10	goulash	**j)**	Italian
11	shish kebob	**k)**	Algonkian
12	dim sum	**l)**	Yiddish
13	pita	**m)**	French

b) Put together a class book of Recipes From Many Cultures. Collect recipes for some of the foods above and others your class is familiar with. You can find recipes from various cultures by: asking classmates whose family is a member of one of the groups, or looking in recipe books in the library. Illustrate your book and make photocopies for each classmate. Try out some of the recipes at home!

Spelling **STRETCH**

20. **Sports Line-up** Words are arranged alphabetically in the dictionary. When looking up words that start with the same letter, look at the letters that follow the first letter (the second, third, fourth, and so on) to figure out where each word would be found in the dictionary. Make a Sports Word Glossary. Arrange the following terms in alphabetical order. Then write a short definition for each. A dictionary will help you. Include pictures if you wish.

striker, centre, home team, draft pick, sportscaster, double, coach, guard, defence, home run, hitter, pitcher, double play, spike, tackle, tight end, dribble

21. **Hink-Pink** A riddle with a rhyming pair of words as the answer is a **hink-pink**. For example: What do you call a large hairpiece? A **big wig**.

a) Use the letters clues to solve these hink-pinks in your notebook:

1 What do you call a baseball player who gained weight?
A _ _ _ _ **er** _ _ **tt** _ _

2 What do you call a distant light in the sky?
A _ **ar** _ _ _ _

3 What do you call a karate champion who lost weight?
A _ _ **gh** _ _ _ **f** _ _ _ **ter**

4 What do you call a fight over a baby's toy?
A _ _ _ _ **le** **b** _ _ _ **le**

b) Write hink-pinks to solve these riddles. What do you call a:

1 delighted father? 2 plump kitten?
3 sliced almond? 4 large swine?
5 fat fish? 6 very unusual couple?

c) Write a riddle for each of the following hink-pink answers.

1 A swap shop 2 A rude dude
3 A fright sight 4 A cold hold

22. Your Point of View

a) Different things have different **points of view**. For example, how might a **shoe** see the world? What might it say if it could talk? It might say something like this:

> "There — my laces are finally tied. I can hardly wait to get walking again!"

> "Must he always walk through puddles? I hate getting wet."

> "I hope she kicks the ball from the side — my front is becoming all scuffed and worn."

Write 3 more things a shoe might say.

b) Complete the following point-of-view paragraph about a rosebush. The first and last lines are given. Write 3 or more sentences to make up the middle of the paragraph.

First line: I certainly hope that she plants me today!

Last line: Now I can stretch out my roots and relax.

c) Pick 1 of these things or use one of your own and write a short paragraph showing the thing's point of view.

    soccer ball   newspaper   tennis racquet

23. If it's a fragment.
The title of this activity is a **sentence fragment**. A fragment is part of a sentence punctuated as if the words form a complete sentence. You should avoid using fragments in formal writing. (Fragments are sometimes okay in informal writing or in dialogue.) You can fix a fragment by adding words to it to make a complete sentence. Or you can change the punctuation so the fragment forms part of the previous sentence. Rewrite the passage on the next page, making it sound more formal by fixing the sentence fragments:

Picnics are no fun. Bugs, dirt, poison ivy. Eating soggy sandwiches. The strawberries squashed at the bottom of the basket. Wouldn't you rather eat in a restaurant? No dishes to clean, no pots to scrub. Usually no bugs around. You can open a window to get some fresh air. If you want fresh air! I prefer air conditioning.

24. **Be a High SCORER!** This strategy will help you do your best on tests in all subjects. It's called SCORER.

S chedule your time. (Look over the whole test and decide how much time you have for each question. Keep working until your time is up.)

C lue words give you help. (Sometimes one question has part of an answer from another question.)

O mit difficult questions. (Mark questions you don't know with an asterisk (*) and come back to them when you have finished the others. Try not to leave any blanks. Write whatever you know.)

R ead directions carefully. (Highlight key direction words. Read difficult questions 3 times.)

E stimate your answers. (Make a guess and ask yourself "Does this make sense?" Check out the value of the question. For example, if it is worth 3 points you should probably include 3 different points in your answer.)

R eview your work. (Read your answers 3 times. Ask yourself: "Is this what I want to say? Does this make sense?")

Copy the test-taking strategy information. Design a card for your desk that reminds you how to be a high SCORER on all your tests. Illustrate it however you wish.

25. What's the Question? This game has a twist! You start with an answer, and then you create 3 questions that fit. For example:

Answer: flashlight

Questions: What's handy to have on a dark night?
What needs batteries to stay bright?
What do you need for reading under the covers?

Select 3 of these answers or write 3 of your own. Write at least 3 questions for each answer. Trade with a partner and see if you can guess each other's answers.

a) toadstool   b) basement   c) pitcher
d) mistake   e) recess   f) monster

26. Dictionary Race To play this dictionary game, you will need a dictionary for each player, 1 die (not 2 dice), and 26 cards with one letter of the alphabet printed on each. The goal of the game is to find a dictionary word that begins with the letter on an alphabet card AND has the same number of letters as the die. Player A begins by turning an alphabet card face-up and rolling the die. All players race to find a word in the dictionary that begins with that letter and has the number of letters on the die. The winner of the round takes the alphabet card. Continue playing until all the cards have been turned over.

27. Quick Change All you need for this game is 2 players, pencil and paper, and word sense.

a) Player A prints a 3- or 4-letter word and hands it to Player B. Player B makes a new word by changing 1 letter in the word. Pass the paper back and forth until a player cannot make any more new words. The last player to make a new word wins the round.

b) Work together to see how many word changes you can make from a single word.

c) Use your new words in interesting sentences. Compare your sentences with a partner.

28. **That's Entertainment!** Use a letter of the alphabet and a theme to make as many entertainment words as you can. Do this for 2 more letter/themes. For example:

A Singers (**A**lanis Morissette)
B Books (**B**abysitters' Club)
E Movies (**E**T)
G TV Shows (**G**oosebumps)
J Actors (**J**im Carrey)
T Groups (**T**ragically Hip)

29. **Cheerio!** Although the people of Great Britain and Canada speak the same language, they use different words for the same things. For example, in Canada we call car fuel **gasoline**. In Britain they say **petrol**. Alison Adams has just arrived in London and she is feeling lost. She doesn't understand some English words everyone around her is using. Look up the British words listed below in the dictionary. Then copy and match the British word to its Canadian meaning to help Alison find her way around London.

British word	Canadian word
1 boot	**a)** ballpoint pen
2 bobby	**b)** checkers
3 cheerio	**c)** sausages and mashed potatoes
4 flat	**d)** elevator
5 mackintosh	**e)** trunk of a car
6 lorry	**f)** police officer
7 draughts	**g)** hello/goodbye
8 bangers and mash	**h)** truck
9 lift	**i)** apartment
10 biro	**j)** raincoat

30. **Word Mobile** List words on a theme (**weather**, **sports**, **foods**) or that start with the same spelling pattern (**sh**, **qu-**, **re-**). Cut out shapes from different colours of construction paper. Hang them from a hanger to make a **mobile**.

31. RIDER This strategy will help you understand descriptive passages that you are reading. By carefully visualizing what you are reading about, you create a detailed picture in your mind. It's called RIDER.

R	ead a sentence.
I	magine a picture of it.
D	escribe the picture to yourself.
E	laborate. Describe the details of clothing, colours, sights, actions, and sounds.
R	epeat steps **R**, **I**, **D**, and **E**.

a) Reread the poem *Thunder and Lightning* on page 52. Use RIDER to visualize the descriptive details. Describe what you see to a partner.

b) Select 1 paragraph from a book you are reading. Use RIDER. Draw a picture of that paragraph. Add as many details as you can.

32. Sound-Alike Sentences
a) Copy and complete this "things-to-do" list by writing a **homophone** (words that sound the same but have different meanings) for each word printed in **bold**.
1 Buy a butterscotch _____ for Ahmed on **Sunday**.
2 Tell the **guest** that you've _____ his age.
3 **I'll** make sure that the boxes don't block the
   _____ .
4 _____ when you hear the neighbour's cat's **paws**.
5 Buy a fishing **reel** made of _____ steel.
6 Tell Lin that I've **seen** a beautiful _____ .
7 Ask Rosa to _____ the canary if she **sees** it fly by.

b) Make up 3 of your own "sound-alike" sentences. Give them to a classmate to complete.

33. **Brainwaves** Does your teacher ever ask you to **brainstorm**? Here is a look at some parts of our body and how the double meanings of words can make them unusual expressions.

kneecap	Where should you wear your knee cap?
shoulder blade	Can the shoulder blade be sharpened?
calf	Will your calf grow up to be a cow?
fingernails	Can a carpenter use your finger nails?

   a) Take these body parts and write questions for them.

      1 funny bone
      2 roof of your mouth
      3 eardrum
      4 palm of your hand
      5 crown of your head
      6 ball of your foot

   b) Draw a small picture to describe each double meaning.

34. **Spelling Banners** Design a banner. On the banner, put a **mnemonic device**. This is a saying, poem, or picture that helps you remember a tricky spelling. For example:

Have a **ball** with a **ball**oon.   You h**ear** with an **ear**.
I'd like to have **2** de**ss**erts.   The princi**pal** is your **pal**.

Share your banner with a partner.

35. **Morse Code** Morse Code uses dots and dashes to send messages. Each letter of the alphabet has its own pattern.
   a) Look carefully at the Morse Code symbols on page 140. Copy the files on the next page in your notebook. Put each letter in the correct file.

continued on the next page ...

A	B
.–	–...
C	D
–.–.	–..
E	F
.	..–.
G	H
––.	....
I	J
..	.–––
K	L
–.–	.–..
M	N
––	–.
O	P
–––	.––.
Q	R
––.–	.–.
S	T
...	–
U	V
..–	...–
W	X
.––	–..–
Y	Z
–.––	––..

1 Letters that are all dots

_____

_____

_____

2 Letters that are all dashes

_____

_____

_____

3 Letters that start with only 1 dot

_____

_____

_____

_____

_____

4 Letters that start with only 1 dash

_____

_____

_____

_____

_____

b) Decode this message using Morse Code:

/ _ / .... / .. / .../ / .. / ... /
/ __ / ___ / .__. / ... / . / / _._. /
___ / _.. / . /

c) Write a short sentence in Morse Code. Trade with a partner and decode each other's sentence.

36. **Pun Fun!** Read these funny names that form phrases. Be sure to exaggerate the pronunciation so you can get the full effect — you may have to read them more than once.

Bud E. System
Jenn U. Wine
Ira Fusa

These imagined books were written by unusual authors. Enjoy the humour and then try some of your own:

A Dog's Life	by Ken L. Keeper
Loving Relationships	by Bea A. Friend
Confessions of a Criminal	by Jules Thief

a) Make up a title for these authors of animal books. Write them in your notebook.

1 _____ by Sally Mander
2 _____ by Al E. Gator
3 _____ by Tadd Pole

b) What kind of books would these authors write?

1 _____ by Eliza Little

2 _____ by B.A. Gardner

3 _____ by Justin Case

c) Now, make up your own funny author and title and illustrate the book cover.

37. Not Just Any BODY

a) Find the **body** words that solve this crossword puzzle. Write them in your notebook.

Across

2 You might tap somebody on this to get his or her attention.

3 You'll find this between your hand and your arm.

5 These carry blood back to the heart.

8 This red liquid moves around inside you.

9 You can feel this to tell how fast your heart is beating.

11 You breathe with these.

12 This pumps **8 Across**.

Down

1 This organ in your head controls everything.

3 Air goes down this pipe.

4 This helps you walk.

6 Here's where your food goes after you swallow.

7 You taste with this.

8 A skeleton is made up of these.

10 This "drum" lets you hear.

141

continued on the next page ...

b) Make your own crossword! Pick a topic you are studying in one of your subjects and choose 10 words that relate to the topic. Arrange the words in different patterns by printing them lightly in pencil on graph paper. When you have a crossing pattern you like, use a pen to outline the boxes around the letters and number the first box of each word. Write a clue for each word. When you are done, erase each word in the puzzle.

c) Share crosswords with your classmates to help each other study the topics.

38. The Backwards Code

a) A secret agent received this coded message:

7 • 19 • 22 | 8 • 11 • 2 | 18 • 8 | 18 • 13 |
12 • 7 • 7 • 26 • 4 • 26.

The next day a mysterious caller phoned and whispered: **4 is W**.
Use this "backwards" code to decode and write the message that the secret agent used.

A	B	C	D	E	F	G	H	I	J	K	L	M
26	25	24	23	22	21	20	19	18	17	16	15	14

N	O	P	Q	R	S	T	U	V	W	X	Y	Z
13	12	11	10	9	8	7	6	5	4	3	2	1

b) Use the "backwards" code to write three sentences in code. Use as many List Words as you can in each sentence. See if a partner can decode your message.

Word List

Words printed in **bold** are **challenge words**.

143